ISBN: 978-1-7347584-9-8

Books by the Author:

Images of America Series…California Missions Book Collection
  The Missions of San Diego
  The Missions of Monterey
  The Missions of San Francisco Bay
  The Missions of Central California
  The Missions of Los Angeles

San Diego UnTapped! … Brewery Tap & Tasting Room Excursions

CALIFORNIA GOLD COUNTRY EXPLORER

©2024 ALL RIGHTS RESERVED
ALL MATERIALS FROM THE AUTHOR'S COLLECTION UNLESS OTHERWISE NOTED

REVISED EDITION

TOUR AND TRAVEL MEDIA
HISTORY • RECREATION • EVENTS
WWW.CALIFORNIATOURANDTRAVEL.COM

CALIFORNIA GOLD COUNTRY EXPLORER

ALL-SEASON TRAVEL TO LEGENDARY SIERRA NEVADA GOLD RUSH MINING TOWNS, TRAILS AND PARKS

CALIFORNIA STATE HIGHWAY 49'S GOLDEN CHAIN VIA SACRAMENTO, LAKE TAHOE, AND YOSEMITE NATIONAL PARK

**FEATURING
A COMPLETE GUIDE TO GOLD PANNING
SETTING UP YOUR OWN MINING CLAIM
AND HUNTING GOLD COUNTRY ANTIQUES!**

**REVISED EDITION
2024**

ROBERT A. BELLEZZA

An 1871 Currier & Ives print commemorating the first transcontinental railroad journey over the Truckee River pass in the Sierra. (Library of Congress)

CALIFORNIA STATEHOOD
1850

BEAR FLAG REPUBLIC
1846

STATE HIGHWAY 49
GOLDEN CHAIN

MAP OF THE GOLDEN STATE

There's a vigorous new generation of 49er residents and an energetic enthusiasm alive in the Sierra Nevada Foothills in support of the traditional values of self-determination and entrepreneurial spirit of past generations. Of the most monumental events shaping the country, the California Gold Rush brought productivity and innovation to a new era of prosperity. An estimated 300,000 streaming into the Golden State with rumors of California nuggets out for the taking created the sudden frenzy that ignited the largest mass migration in recorded history. In 1849, the pilgrimage began by wagon, horse, mule, oxen, or on foot to bring prospectors to the Sierra Nevada from all corners of the globe.

Today, the Gold Country region displays hundreds of old brick-and-mortar buildings of the 1849 Gold Rush with nearly 500 established mining towns. The Gilded Age produced more efficient water systems, steam power generation, long-line electrical transmission, long-distance telephone lines, new clothing styles, expansive agricultural methods, and other innovations. By 1869, the crowning achievement celebrated the arrival of the first transcontinental railroad in Sacramento, at the confluence of the American and Sacramento rivers. A common thread connects much more than mining, lumber, status, or wealth but conveys a sense of commitment to its verdant landscape and the authentic era of 49er pioneering hospitality.

Exploration and travel on California State Highway 49 leads to the most panoramic foothill destinations in the Sierra Nevada foothills along a 300-mile journey north to south. Entering the majestic California State Parks of the Sierra foothills, visitors discover wooded landscapes and steep canyons of moderate to mountainous terrain and access to unlimited recreational opportunities. Most certainly, there is never a dull moment touring State the Highway 49 Golden Chain and visiting the museum-quality mining towns, living history events, campouts, trails, and adventures following its legendary pioneering history.

Acknowledgment
An American Biography
Leaves of Silver and Gold

Across the western slope of the Sierra Nevada Mountains, his quest of the 'Range of Light' was the object of relentless study by John Muir, on his arrival to California in 1868. As a resident scholar of the "Institute of the Wilderness", his studies of Arctic glaciers and seeing their indelible effects on the mountainous regions of Alaska intrigued Muir by the visible glacial scarring seemingly evident throughout Yosemite. With a vigorous and consistent advocacy to championing national parklands, he pointed his efforts toward Yosemite, Lake Tahoe, and the other regions of conservation within the Sierra Nevada. His vision established the Sierra Club. During the Gold Rush years, the watershed lands of the foothills and valleys in California became more polluted from the continuous exposure of mining wastes into intricate systems of rivers and streams. In the 1880s, hazardous conditions became more visible, and protests had arisen against widespread and uncontrolled hydraulic mining contamination of valley soils and declaring the practice a disaster in court. The momentous Sawyer decision ruling in favor of agriculture, forever banned the practice of hydraulic mining and permanently closed all these surface mines. The California law became among the first environmental laws in governing the degradation of its public lands.

John Olmsted, 21st Century pioneer conservationist.

John de Vaux Olmsted (March 2, 1938–March 8, 2011), an environmental warrior and tenacious ecologist with imposing views promoting John Muir's concepts of accessibility in public lands, created the handicapped recreational zones on the Independence Trail of Yuba River South Fork with his unique ingenuity. Opening September 16, 2007, as a California State Park and expanded to 11,000 acres, the trailhead at the Nevada City Highway 49 Yuba River crossing, high above the mighty river's edge he engineered elevated boardwalks and followed the old wooden water flume meandering 2.2 miles, exposing the beauty of the natural Yuba canyon river landscapes for wheelchair hikers and all visitors. In his earlier life, John Olmsted was the first Education Director at Golden Gate Park, and a teacher with the Oakland Museum

Natural Science Docents program. His idea of a 300-mile cross-state outdoor museum began in 1969 and resulted in his leadership study of California State Highway 20 at Chico State University. His project identified the rare Stairstep Pygmy Forest terrain for miles along Highway 20, ending at the Fort Bragg oceanfront. At the time, bulldozers stationed at the Pacific Ocean's beach threatened immediate development of the area, gratefully was halted when a cold year's snowfall fell over the town, just in time for John's intervention. The outcome was decided by the State in favor of John's efforts granting the establishment of Jug Handle State Park at Fort Bragg beach. John's landmark parks and trails have included preserving wildlife and flora species along State Highway 20, and at Discovery Trail near the Lake Spaulding Campground.

Sniffing a fragrant Scotch Pine in July.

With recognition from author Gretel Ehrlich in her National Geographic publication, John Muir – Nature's Visionary, she cites Olmsted as a significant contemporary environmental figure with his photo gracing the last page next to one of John Muir. This edition, Sierra Nevada Explorer gratefully acknowledges John Olmsted's tour of the Yuba-Donner National Scenic Byway, on the 160-mile loop along California State Highways 20, 49, and 89 in Sierra County to Donner Lake, Truckee, and Nevada City. John was a lifelong conservationist, humorist, self-taught raconteur, recycler, preservationist, and a friend always beaming with the love of fellow man, botany, and wildlife. His rise to prominence made him a noteworthy trailblazer and cultural patriot of his time.

Those fine attributes were proven one Fourth of July weekend in 2009, after our meeting at the Yosemite Le Conte Lodge attending a book signing for author Bonnie Gisel's 'Kindred Spirits' on the correspondence of John Muir. Afterwards, Olmsted suggested we blaze a hiking trail straight up the rim wall from Le Conte Lodge. Departing after the book signing, we started our ascent with John's steady determination switching back and forth bush-whacking on near vertical trails, as the Valley Floor disappeared well beneath our feet. Midway, John paused to recount the story of John Muir hugging a rotund Scotch Pine and inhaling the aroma of butterscotch, then in the warmth of the hot July sun, reenacting Muir's story at a nearby tree. And, with a glimpse towards the Valley below framed by the distant plumes of Bridal Veil Fall whitewater waving wildly in the wind, I felt eternally grateful for that moment and John's efforts in preserving the memory of those fragile vapors.

14 TOURS IN THE SIERRA NEVADA FOOTHILLS

CONTENTS

CALIFORNIA GOLD COUNTRY MAP	... 7
THE GOLDEN STATE MAP	... 8
PREFACE	... 9
ACKNOWLEDGMENTS	... 10
CONTENTS	... 12
CALIFORNIA STATE HIGHWAY 49	... 19
CALIFORNIA GOLD RUSH STATE PARKS	... 27
MAP OF CALIFORNIA GOLD MINES	... 28
THE GOLD STANDARD	... 29
1849 MINING DISTRICTS OF CALIFORNIA	... 30
CALIFORNIA'S NATIVE AMERICANS	... 31

I. SACRAMENTO GOLD COUNTRY

1. SUTTER'S FORT TO SUTTER'S MILL ... 37
Begin a tour from the earliest California Gold Rush settlement at Sutter's Fort State Historic Park, and take in the journey along the American River to Sutter's Mill and discovery site at Marshall Gold Discovery State Historic Park, where the first golden nuggets were found on the American River South Fork. Discover the museums, living history events, and wildflower trails.

2. OLD SACRAMENTO WALKING TOURS ... 45
With over 55 California Gold Rush era landmark buildings in view, Old Sacramento State Historic Park follows a tour from the waterfront at the iconic Tower Bridge, the Delta King Riverboat, Firehouse Alley, to largest regional museum of its kind, the California State Railroad Museum and Railyard at Front and I Streets. Old Sacramento features over 30 diversified museums.

3. SACRAMENTO TO OLD FOLSOM ... 61
Visit Sutter Street in Old Folsom, 23 miles east of Sacramento on US Highway 50. From downtown Old Folsom on an American River and Lake Natoma tour, visit the historic Folsom Powerhouse, Folsom Lake, American River Bike Trail, and the spectacular destination shops and restaurants in the area.

The Big Four railroad magnates offices centered in Old Sacramento currently house museums adjacent to the California State Railroad Museum and Firehouse Alley.

4. Sacramento to Placerville ... 66

Downtown Placerville was an early Gold Rush tent camp located just 10 miles north of the Sutter's Mill gold discovery site on the American River. Originally named Old Hangtown, the old mining town has over 90 historical homes, buildings, shops, and features the 60-acre Gold Bug Mine Park, Stamp Mill and mining tour. Make stops at Diamond Springs, Camino, Fair Play, the vineyards, wineries, breweries, Apple Hill farms, and fresh-cut Christmas tree farms.

II. Northern Sierra Nevada Foothills

5. Exploring the 'Lake Of The Sky' ... 75

Lake Tahoe, the largest alpine mountain lake of North America is located within three Gold Country counties, with the lake divided in half vertically by the geographical Nevada State line. A landmark freshwater lake often referred to as 'Tahoe Blue' and 'Lake Of The Sky' is 122,600 surface acres. Historically, Tahoe is a well-known destination crossroads center of activity, entertainment, water sports, boating, biking, hiking, and thrilling ski trips.

6. Old Auburn Crossroads ... 80

32 miles east on I-80 from Sacramento at the Nevada Street Exit and historic downtown Auburn, visit a significant crossroads destination of mining and railroading. Downtown Auburn is near the towns of Foresthill, Colfax, Dutch Flat and several traditional stopovers on the way to Lake Tahoe. Continue south on Highway 49 to the Auburn Ravine State Recreational Area, stretching 40 miles along the North and Middle Forks of the American River.

7. NEVADA CITY & GRASS VALLEY GETAWAY ... 86

Continue north of Auburn from the I-80 exit, 23 miles on State Highway 49 towards Grass Valley and its sister town Nevada City, in the Northern Mining Region. Visitors enjoy the colorful Gold Rush towns of covered walkways, museums, living history events, early stone and brick buildings, with celebratory parades, unique shops, lodging, restaurants, and surrounding recreational possibilities. Highway 49 is a starting point to touring the Yuba-Donner Scenic Byway and the Truckee, Lake Tahoe, and Reno area.

8. YUBA DONNER NATIONAL SCENIC BYWAY ... 99

Take in the scenery of three Gold Country counties along the 160-mile Yuba-Donner National Scenic Byway and Highway 49. Begin in Nevada City and meander through rustic Gold Rush mining towns and explore the byway's Yuba River trailheads. Explore the Alleghany Mine and Kentucky Mine Stamp Mill museums, Sierra Buttes, Downieville Gold Lakes region, Tahoe-Donner Lake Pass and landmark sites of the tragic plight of early wagon trains.

9. GOLD LAKES BASIN & SIERRA VALLEY ...116

Access high-country recreational destinations on State Highway 49 in Plumas and Sierra Counties at the historic mining towns of Downieville, Gold Lake, Sierra City, Sierraville, Loyalton, Blairsden, and Portola. Discover over 50 high-elevation lakes in the Gold Lakes Basin with recreational skiing, golfing resorts, wildflowers, rafting, fishing, boating, swimming, biking and camping. Tour the Alleghany Sixteen-to-One Mine and Kentucky Mining Museum on Highway 49.

The Sierra Snow Plant.

III. Central Sierra Nevada Foothills

10. Amador Mining & Agriculture ... 133

From downtown Sacramento via State Highway 16, travel east to the State Highway 49 connection in Amador County, just south of the El Dorado Foothill Wine Country. Enter the Amador Shenandoah Valley vineyard region from the gateway town of Plymouth. Follow the 49er Golden Chain to Amador County's mining and agriculture in Drytown, Amador City, Sutter Creek, Volcano, and Jackson. Tour the Kennedy Mine, Mining Wheels, Knight Foundry, historical museums, restaurants, antique stores, art, and gift shops while enjoying surrounding seasonal recreational opportunities. At the junction of Highway 49 and State Highway 88 discover the resorts of Silver Lake, Caples Lake, and Kirkwood on a scenic highway leading to South Lake Tahoe.

11. The Golden Path Of History ... 151

A tour of Calaveras County begins on the Golden Chain of Highway 49 at the Mother Lode mining town of San Andreas, and courthouse where the famous stage robber Black Bart stood trial. Visit nearby Mokelumne Hill and distinctive Gold Rush center near the Mokelumne River. Further south on Highway 49, explore Angels Camp, an original tent camp and home to the Celebrated Jumping Frog Jubilee. The festive event is relived every year for visitors and residents. A scenic drive on Highway 49 east via State Highway 4 leads to the Giant Sequoia Redwoods at Calaveras Big Trees Park, with over 6,000 acres of redwood trees up to 25-feet in diameter. Visit the Gold Rush towns of Murphys, Arnold, Avery, Vallecito, Carson Hill, and further north to Bear Valley and Ebbetts Pass surrounded by camping, biking, high-altitude fishing and unlimited choices of vacation resorts.

California Red Poppy.

IV. SOUTHERN SIERRA NEVADA FOOTHILLS

12. THE SOUTHERN MINES ... 167

California Lupines.

The Southern Mines region of the Gold Country includes the colorful mining towns and museums of Tuolumne County. Gold Rush destinations include Columbia State Historic Park, and Jamestown at 1897 Railtown.Follow State Highway 49 along the Golden Chain to the picturesque mining towns of Sonora, Twain Harte, Pinecrest, Tuttletown, Mt. Bullion, Chinese Camp and Groveland, to the Big Oak Flat access at nearby Yosemite Park. Travelers discover numerous recreational possibilities including choices of water sports at lakes, houseboating, fishing, whitewater rafting, trail hiking, golfing, swimming and rock climbing.

13. THE YOSEMITE GATEWAY ... 181

Discover Mariposa County on Highway 49's Golden Chain from the gateway of El Portal, following State Highway 140 along the Merced River to the entrance of Yosemite National Park. Visit the unique Gold Rush town in downtown Mariposa on Highway 49, and explore historical memorabilia at the Mariposa History Center, Mariposa Courthouse, and California State Mining Museum. In Coulterville at the Highway 49 junction of County Highway J132, take State Highway 120 past the Hetch Hetchy Valley Reservoir into the Yosemite National Park entry gate at Big Oak Flat. Highway 120 traverses the entire park, passing by the Tuolumne and Merced Grove of Giant Sequoias into Yosemite Valley, and connects to the eastern gate at Tuolumne Meadows on Tioga Road, ending at US Highway 395 near Mono Lake.

14. YOSEMITE NATIONAL PARK ... 189

Explore the southern Gold Country from Oakhurst at the terminus of State Highway 49 from Highway 41. Just 14 miles east at the southern entry gate of Yosemite National Park are historical destinations with spectacular day trips at the Mariposa Sequoia Grove with the oldest known Giant Sequoia Redwood, the Grizzly Giant. Visit the nearby destinations at Coarsegold, Bass Lake, North Fork, Ahwahnee, Fish Camp, Yosemite Mountain Sugar Pine Railroad, Sierra Vista Byway, and Yosemite at the Wawona Lodge, with the 9-hole Sierra Golf Course, Yosemite History Center, Badger Ski Resort, Inspiration Point, Glacier Point, Yosemite Valley, El Capitan, and Half Dome.

V. CALIFORNIA GOLD RUSH & US STATEHOOD

CALIFORNIA HISTORICAL TIMELINE BETWEEN **1848-1850** ... **216**

VI. PICK AND PANS

GOLD COUNTRY ANTIQUE HUNTING ... **219**

GUIDE TO GOLD PANNING ... **223**

ADDENDUM
CHAPTER INDEX ... **228**

AUTHOR STORYBOARD ... **230**

California Wild Iris.

California Golden Poppy.

View of the American River from Highway 49 at the Auburn Ravine State Recreation Area, 17 miles from the Marshall Gold Discovery State Park.

CALIFORNIA STATE HIGHWAY 49
THE GOLD RUSH OF 1849

WAY OUT WEST

If you've not traveled California State Highway 49 and the scenic Gold Country foothills of the Sierra Nevada Mountain Range, there is a more than likely prospect of having heard about 'The California Gold Rush of 1849' and the famous Eureka! It was an incredible moment in America propelling the most significant mass migration in recorded history.

A CALIFORNIA GOLD HUNTER MEETING A SETTLER.
(Library of Congress)

In the Winter of 1848, the American River's surging waters settling after a hard winter's rain, furthered the completion constructing a water-powered sawmill on the riverbank in Coloma. James W. Marshall diverted the river's thrust into a raceway to power an oversized waterwheel with belting connecting the sawblade and the log carriage overhead on the raised platform. Needing increased efficiency in the mill race, he decided to use John Sutter's 10-man crew and a group of eight native Indians to dam the forebay and cleared the obstructions. Inspecting the channel and walking the extent of the race, he stopped to glance down seeing two glimmering pennyweight nuggets as the work crew looked on, as the 38-year-old New Jersey native made a discovery of shiny gold in a pool of water. On his return to Sacramento and meeting with his Swiss-German partner, John Augustus Sutter, each man faced the reality that their lives at Sutter's Fort had changed forever.

John Sutter established Sutter's Fort in 1839 as the original regional settlement. It became a provincial outpost and favorite stopover for frontier travelers to rest within its fortress-thick walls. Previously, Sutter retained the land through a sizable Mexican grant with his repatriation as a Mexican citizen. A sizable sense of nobility and gregarious manner, he brought good relationships, and called as 'Captain Sutter' to all who knew him. He built an historic fort by the Sacramento River and compensated local Indians generously, and offered fresh horses and livestock whenever visited by guests, travelers, and fur trapping expeditions. After meeting James Wilson Marshall, Sutter offered him a place to stay in trade for work, agreeing to a partnership in constructing a large sawmill at Coloma, 35 miles away. At first, the sawmill project gave Marshall and Sutter some personal gain selling off shares of the mill. With the sawmill ready by August, Marshall made the remarkable discovery of gold the following year, on January 24, 1848.

Spreading like wildfire, rumors of finding gold stirred thousands of Americans to the rallying cry, 'There's Gold In Them Hills!' The fervor for gold created a stampede of settlers to the tent camps around Coloma, Hangtown, Folsom, Auburn, and Plymouth with numbers increasing in arrivals. Sensational tales heard by migrants would turn imaginations into wild hysteria, as both the young and old landed on the San Francisco shores. Of the multitudes of goldseekers overflowing the streets, each man procured the tools, food, clothing, wagons, horses, mules, and oxen and began a solemn two-hundred-mile trail into the Sacramento Valley at Sutter's Fort, and proceed to where there was no trail. Prospectors encountering steep canyons, glistening rivers, and untouched rolling foothills, following the trails trodden by the Gold Rush forty-niners. Thirty-five miles upstream from Sacramento along the American River, the hills radiated with talk of lucrative returns and the news of gold for the taking. Over 300,000 migrants attracted to the lure of an unknown destiny, arrived after thousands of miles to explore the mythical rivers and streams. Gold prospectors lived where they worked, on the riverbanks in tent camps staking out claims on a quest to find the elusive, precious mineral.

Westward Ho! (Library of Congress)

"Go West, Young Man" had manifested the inner primal urge to conquering one's destiny and the vision of finding unimaginable wealth in California. Explorations towards the wilderness wending the way of prospectors along river gorges and mountainous paths gave rise with odd monikers describing a remote location, a daily event, or quirky personality. The camps coined the names You Bet, Caldwell's Upper Store, Rough & Ready, Timbuctoo, Amador, Twain Harte, Rich Bar, Angels, Nevada, Fiddletown, Wild Yankee, Sonorian, Dry Creek Diggins, French Corral, and Malakoff Diggins, some with more daunting names, First Garrote, changed to Groveland. Another famous tent camp, 15 miles east of Sutter's Mill, had ominous fame as Hangtown, then transformed to Placerville in 1850. A vital crossroads into Coloma, west of Sacramento, and east of the Emigrant Trail over the Sierra Nevada, the world rushed in huge numbers lured by an irresistible magnetism and the golden

After the California Gold Rush, John A. Sutter retired near penniless. (Library of Congress)

promises more often than not, an adventure receiving a fate of an empty-handed fortune! As the rivers panned out early in the 1850s and lucrative placer strikes slowly dried, and fewer nuggets randomly discovered, miners began a fabled fortune of well beneath the ground, unified as a giant 'Mother Lode' with its tennacles in different directions. Envisioning the abundance of gold in potential miles, the celebrated 'Mother Lode' was calculated to be approximately four miles wide at a distance nearly 120 miles long, northwest to southeast, touching the boundaries of El Dorado, Amador, Calaveras, Tuolumne, and Mariposa Counties. Later, many operations were joined to make impressive conglomerates, developing storybook successes during a newly found Gilded Age. By the 1850s, with extensive use of water and steam, omnipresent thundering-stamp mills were driven by powerful gravity-fed streams of water lifting near 1000lb hefty hammers to crush lode ore. Another method to exposing the surface aggregate of ancient riverbeds close to the ground level had developed into a practice called 'Hydraulicking' from the use of high-pressured gravity-fed water from the mountains, feeding tapered nozzles called monitors and the power to washing silt, trees, and rocks. Carrying the heaviest aggregates, gravel, ore, and black sand into giant sluice boxes, the tumultuous hydraulicking process began spreading into mining towns claiming mineral recovery over entire landscapes, and eventually entirely banned. Massive industrial dredging operations harnessed immense mechanical shovels spanning entire riverbeds to claw and scrape boulders away, down to granite bedrock. Diversionary tunnels were drilled into rock and diverted water into ditches through steel and wooden flumes, and sent over elaborate trestles spanning over mountain canyons. Torrents of water washed and sluiced the aggregate to the finest grains, then the gold production process was completed using mercury as an amalgam.

Within the Central Mines Region in 1848, new placer discoveries brought exciting reports of a 75-pound placer gold nugget discovered in Jamestown at Woods Creek, and discoveries of large bounties in gold panning at the nearby Columbia Basin. Mining shifted underground after extracting deposits below bedrock, and by 1859, the ore mined from the Central Mother Lode area exceeded 13,300,000 ounces. In the Northern Mining region of Grass Valley, miners discovered ledges of translucent quartz drifts embedded with gold ore veins at deep levels. The Empire Mine reached 11,000 feet and ran into the 1950s, becoming one of few deepest California Mines. A decade later, designated an important Gold Rush Historic Park and surrounding

"Hydrauliking" in French Corral used torrents of high-pressure gravity-fed water shot from 'monitors'. The practice became widespread exposing ancient tertiary river beds. (Library of Congress)

woodlands, trails, and landscapes provide a glimpse of visible former foundation walls throughout the 800 acre park. The extensive equipment yard and workshops include an assay office, yard office, elevator shaft, and giant headframe. Within a setting of gardens and landscaped forested hills are beautifully the designed rock buildings, courtyard and greenhouse, with the Summer residence of the Empire Mine owner. Over half of all gold deposits from the Gold Rush were produced by the sister towns from the Empire Mine in Grass Valley and its neighboring mining town, Nevada City, given the title 'Queen City of the Northern Mines. Together, they are the largest producing regional area of historical California gold. By 1859, the Empire accumulated lode gold ore totals equaling 10,400,000 ounces, and 2,200,000 ounces of placer gold. By 1860, nearly 750,000 pounds of gold mined was valued at the time a mere $12 to $35 an ounce. In comparison, the total in 2007 from all California gold production was 90,000 ounces derived from only two sources, the Mesquite Mine in Imperial County and the Briggs Mine, a reprocessing mine in Inyo County.

Mexico's Eroding Power

In the 1790s, a population of Americans settled in California were living among indigenous natives, the missions with Spanish friars, colorful conquistadors, and merchants. Groups of fur traders, mountain men, mariners, and US military soldiers arriving in the West during the 1820s led to eventual American industries and robust trading along the Pacific seaports with around 500 settlers. During 1827, Monterey, capital of Alta, with a wide harbor at the center of California coastal commerce, served the inward and outward-bound supply ships. As the Mexico City government grappled with the numbers of American migrants, orders had been sent enforcing all foreigners to vacate the territory of Alta California.

A distinguished American, William B. Ide, a settler in the upper Sacramento Valley, organized a group of men of over thirty soldiers under the independent rebellion named 'The Bear Flag Revolt', in 1846. These loyal Americans flew the flag of the California Republic and rode into Sonoma Square under surprise attack on June 14, 1846. The Bear Flag signaled the urge of Americans for independence from Mexico, and its loosely held government. Made from a single piece of white cloth and designed by William Todd, the flag displayed a crude symbolic Grizzly Bear with one star in the upper corner and a wide red stripe across the bottom. The flag was unfurled at the Bear Flag Revolt against the Mexican headquarters in Sonoma, and then arresting the retired General Mariano Guadalupe Vallejo at his home with his family, Americans confiscated nine brass cannons and over 250 guns. The attackers issued a proclamation declaring California an independent Republic. Although retired and residing in Sonoma, Vallejo was somewhat sympathetic to the Americans, but still was kept under guard at Sutter's Fort and consigned as a prisoner of war for two months.

General Mariano Guadalupe Vallejo, commander of the Mexican military.

By July 7, 1846, John D. Sloat, Commodore of the US Naval Pacific Squadron, took command of the Capital of Monterey and stood unopposed in raising the US Flag. He began taking control of San Francisco and the surrounding towns, and the momentum of the war and continued with bloody battles in Monterey, Mexico, in September 1846, and finally, San Pasquale in San Diego, in less than two years ending with victory by the Americans. The Treaty of Guadalupe Hildago on February 2, 1848 ceded 525,000 square miles of the western frontier with Alta California awarded as part of the United States acquisitions and included present-day Arizona, Colorado, Nevada, New Mexico, Utah, and Wyoming. After the impact of the 1846 Bear Flag Revolt was settled, many Americans were the first to hear about the 1848 Gold Discovery at the beginning of the Gold Rush. The final movement to Statehood, as the 31st in the Union, was duly ratified by an act of the US Congress on September 9, 1850.

THE RIVERS OF GOLD
President Polk described the news of California discoveries during the State of the Union Address. Tall frigates departed the shores transiting nearly 3,000 miles over the Atlantic Ocean 'around the horn' and completing a trip

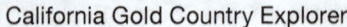

The Kennedy Tailing Wheels Park exhibit on display in Martell, with two of four original 58-foot diameter wooden wheels from 1914. Once covered in tin sheds, the wheels were engineered to lift uphill piles of silt and tailings to an impound dam, at Indian Gulch. Today, the wheels are iconic reminders of mining's reliance on water and the challenges of modern innovation and invention during the Gold Rush era.

to San Francisco in 89 days. Necessities of provisions, food, lodging, camping, and mining gear were sold in immense quantities to make Sam Brannan the first successful California millionaire. Well before the first waves of migrants, he had invested in buying all the available picks, shovels, and hardware in San Francisco. His supply stores were outfitted for Gold Rush arrivals, and he sold goods at three strategic hubs, in San Francisco, Sutter's Fort, and Coloma. Henry Wells and William Fargo moved 'Out West' and opened security and assay offices. A German-born tailor, Levi Strauss, arrived in San Francisco in 1850 opening supply stores selling canvas tarps and wagon coverings to the miners. In 1852, John Studebaker manufactured wheelbarrows and buggy wheels for farmers and miners. Phillip Armour founded a meatpacking empire in Chicago and traveled West, then operated the sources for water in the high Sierra controlling the goldfields during the Gold Rush and sold sluicing processes, separating gold ore from the coarse aggregate. A poke of gold dust became the daily currency at tent camps. Eggs, once a dollar rose to $8 after spiraling costs, and a pound of coffee sold for $40. More 'modern' progress brought the transcontinental Central Pacific Railroad and the first trains in the summer of 1869, arriving over the Sierra Nevada near Donner Pass and opening the main route of travel from eastern destinations 20 years after the Gold Rush.

HIDDEN GOLD

The treasures of the Sierra Nevada today include its scenic wildlife in natural surroundings and verdant landscapes. The seasonal Fall foliage of the Sierra foothills illuminates hardwood forests in vivid displays found throughout the 49 Golden Chain. Steep canyons and forests with lush panoramas await along the old State Highway 49 from Nevada and Sierra Counties and the 'Sierra Scenic National Byway' through Gold Rush towns of tall steeples, Victorian architecture, boardwalks, and tall gables shedding winter snows. Further explorations along Highway 49 enjoy the sightings of a lone bald eagle riding the thermals, an off-chance booking of a rafting trip, or a cruise on a houseboat. Incredible migrations in the hundreds of thousands made the 1849 Gold Rush a worldwide phenomenon, etched permanently in the annals of American history. Green State California State Highway signs represent a silhouetted miners' shovel staked symbolically into the ground, honoring the California Gold Rush 'forty-niners'.

A satirical look at the novice Gold Rush miner, by H. R. Robinson. (Library of Congress)

1849 MINING DESTINATONS IN CALIFORNIA

THE NORTHERN MINES

The northern destinations of Plumas, Sierra, and Nevada counties transit over canyons of the Yuba and Feather rivers and to several mining towns on the Sierra National Scenic Byway. The 160-mile circuitous byway loop passes near Truckee, Donner Pass and Lake Tahoe, using Highways I-80, 20, 49, and 89. In Sierra City, the Kentucky Mine Museum displays a cache of mining equipment and sponsors annual events at the park's amphitheater.

In Alleghany, the 1896 Sixteen-To-One Mine mining museum and underground tours are near wide rivers with over 50 cool mountain lakes found around the towns of Blairsden, Graeagle, Downieville, Bassetts, Goodyear, Camptonville, North San Juan, and Truckee gateway into the Sierra Nevada recreational region. Grass Valley and Nevada City are considered the largest producing California Gold Rush mining regions.

THE CENTRAL MOTHER LODE

Central Gold Country along State Highway 49, intersects with Highways 4, 12, 16, 50, 88, 108, 120, and 140 and continues north to south through Plymouth, Drytown, Amador City, Fiddletown, Volcano, Sutter Creek, Jackson, San Andreas, Mokelumne, Murphys, and Angels Camp passing by landmark mines, unique museums, foothill vineyards, Victorian homes, antique brick and masonry buildings once inhabited by luminaries such as Mark Twain, Bret Harte, John Muir, and several visiting US Presidents. A Native American Pow Wow held at Chaw'se Indian Grinding Rock State Historic Park is celebrated each May in Pine Grove. The Calaveras Jumping Frog Jubilee perpetuates Mark Twain's famous tale. Mining tours at Kennedy Mine in Jackson and include outdoor displays of immense wooden Mine Tailing Wheels in nearby Martell. East of Highway 49 leads to more primitive areas on Highway 4 and include trailheads at the Calavaras Big Trees Park. Highway 88, to South Lake Tahoe, passes by Silver Lake, Caples Lake, and Kirkwood resorts in the High Sierra.

THE SOUTHERN GOLD COUNTRY

Highway 49 leads to Yosemite National Park, travelers pass Don Pedro Lake and New Melones Reservoir and unlimited choices of recreational resources on the southern Golden Chain. Make a stop at Mark Twain's cabin just off Jackass Road. Proceed to Columbia State Historic Park, Sonora, and Jamestown, each well-preserved mining towns from the Gold Rush era. Highway 49 continues toward Mariposa's switchback ascent through the steep Merced River Canyon to Oakhurst. From Highway 49's southern terminus, it is a short drive north taking Highway 41 to southern Yosemite. The road also leads to side trips in Fish Camp, Bass Lake, the Nelder Grove, the Yosemite Sugar Pine Railroad, North Fork at the California geographical center, the Sierra Vista Scenic Byway and Mariposa Grove of Giant Sequoias.

Gold Rush State Historic Parks

The 49er Golden Chain Highway beside the surging waters of the American River South Fork, extends through the rustic valley setting of Coloma, between Auburn and Placerville. Of five official Gold Rush Parks, the 576-acre Marshall Gold Discovery State Historic Park, and site of the 1849 Gold Rush, tells the founding story of gold discovery where James Marshall and John Sutter stepped into history, on the banks of the American River at Sutter's Mill. At the site, a replicated sawmill was built close to where Marshall found two small nuggets in January of 1848. Visitors enjoy gold panning, buggy rides, or a stroll on wildflower trails near the river, and absorb the authentic forty-niner history with its original buildings and serene foothill valley surroundings. At the center of the historic mining town are a museum, blacksmith shop, homes, schoolhouse, jailhouse, horse and buggy stable, plus several 'Living History' events.

The Coloma Valley, Highway 49 and site of the gold discovery, on the American River.

Gold Rush parks include the Northern District's Plumas-Eureka State Historic Park, Malakoff Diggins Historic Park, and Empire Mine State Historic Park, with each representing more than half the total gold mined during the California Gold Rush. The Central and Southern Mines follow the Mother Lode trail along Highway 49 over 80 miles, the Golden Chain from Coloma to Sonora. In Columbia State Historic Park the original Gold Rush Wells Fargo office with stagecoach rides and a gold panning diggins, features a blacksmith shop, theater, firehouse, curio shops, hotels, and living history events within the town of brick buildings, porticoes and boardwalks in a complete, well-preserved mining town. The Central Mining towns are perfect getaways for those in search of restaurants, lodging, waterwater rafting and recreational spots. In the southern Sierra lasting into the late 19th Century, Bodie State Historic Park in Bridgeport, California, has the last great Gold Rush destination of a remote ghost town nestled far into the high mountains, at the 8,375-foot elevation. This famous mining town known for its wild west lifestyle of ill-repute, continued as a busy gold and silver center until the early 20th Century. A trip to Bodie is a worthwhile adventure to the center of a still and serene ghost town. It was the last of the great mining town legends!

Map of Gold Mines in California

The term 'Mother Lode' describes an assumption of an underground interconnected series of gold-bearing quartz veins, as visualized in the miners' imagination to be located from the American River extending to a point in Mariposa. The working miners ascertained the veins of ore as the Lode's 'tentacles', radiating as offspring.

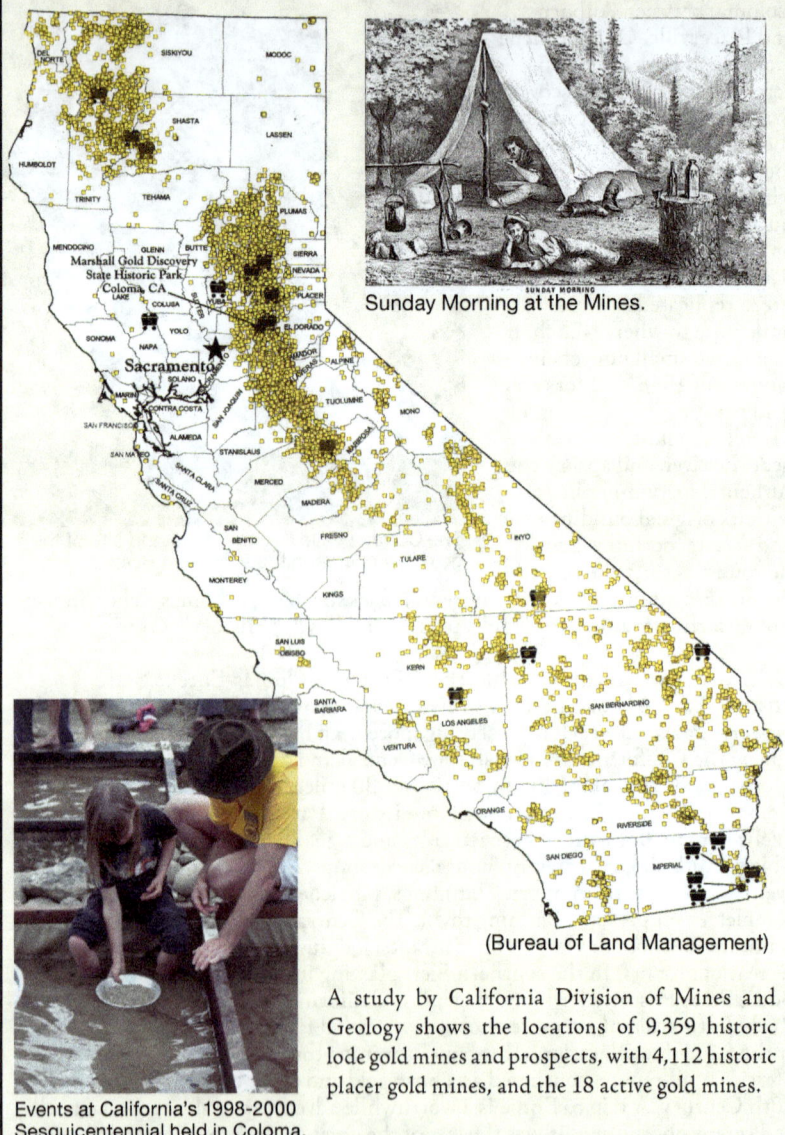

Sunday Morning at the Mines.

(Bureau of Land Management)

Events at California's 1998-2000 Sesquicentennial held in Coloma.

A study by California Division of Mines and Geology shows the locations of 9,359 historic lode gold mines and prospects, with 4,112 historic placer gold mines, and the 18 active gold mines.

THE GOLD STANDARD
STATE HIGHWAY 49

Like the spokes of an old wagon wheel spinning from its center, the California Gold Country regions interconnecting crossroads with meandering circuitous trails, encompass vast territories equaling one-fifth of the entire Golden State. The forty-niner State Highway extends across the western slope of the Sierra Foothills and takes travelers along a vertical axis of 300 miles, north and south. Throughout the Sierra Nevada, travelers encounter frequent spectacular regional rivers, streams, lakes and wildlife sightings. Easy to begin anywhere on a 'Golden Triangle' from Sacramento, Lake Tahoe, and Yosemite National Park and to Sierra Nevada touring elevations ranging from 900 to 2,500 feet, or much higher.

Visitors find remote backroad trails with serene lakes, wild rivers, streams, valleys, and steep mountainous terrain.

Beneath the surface, the Mother Lode traces the path of pioneer prospectors into the legendary Gold Rush mining centers, leading them along trails to establishing tent camps at placer and hard rock mines, in the lively foothill communities of a new Gilded Age of America. Mining claims lined the riverbanks and placer mines harnessed strong river currents via water flumes powering waterwheels, elevated rockers, and sluices called the Long Tom, washing and sifting out gold dust. Hardrock underground mining began the 1850s with new migrations into the California mining areas, and the 1849 Gold Rush continued its lure of gold into the foothill mining towns, established like the 'beads on a golden necklace', along a Golden Chain of nearly 500 original Gold Rush towns along the earliest trails of the forty-niners.

Ore carts at Empire Mine, Grass Valley.

An original Pelton Waterwheel at Northstar Mining Museum, Grass Valley.

CALIFORNIA NATIVE AMERICANS
THE INDIGENOUS NATIVES OF THE SIERRA NEVADA

Lucy Parker in 2003, resident of Mono County and native Yosemite Miwok-Paiute. (Dan Barta)

Of Native American tribal legends, the names Nisenan, Miwok, Paiute, and Maidu were the original people inhabiting the ridges, streams, and lakes among foothill golden oaks and tall pines. Yokut, Valley Maidu, Wintun, and Miwok were spread throughout the Sacramento and San Joaquin Valleys. Yurok, Karok, and Hupa resided in the dark canyons under the Redwoods. Costanoan, Chumash and Pomo populations lived along the coastal regions, known as stewards of the lush forests and rolling hills for over nine millennia. The natives had little to do as warriors, but rather were the gatherers of acorns, fishermen, and basket weavers with cultural skills that survived during the unsettled years of California. Peace pervaded the region for 1000s of years, abruptly unraveled when Spanish Missionaries' domination as colonizers had first settled California in San Diego, beginning in 1769. The eastern states of America bringing explorers, fur traders, and settlers to California during the early 19th century, with over 300,000 migrants streaming into the Sierra Nevada, the impact of the California Gold Rush immediately caused upheavals beyond imagination, and tore apart the forest vegetation, felling trees, polluted the streams, and washed away hillsides with hydraulic mining. In Yosemite, indigenous Miwok were dispersed, losing their heritage over the years, as many tribes suffered disastrous conflicts with miners and were unprotected from diseases of European origins, causing nearly a 90% reduction in their populations. They have been remembered, and today many tribes live in peace welcoming visitors to their tribal pow wows and continue to display the cultural diversity they once lived.

The 'tiny' oak acorn has fed and nourished native Americans for centuries, and probably millennia. In California, the original inhabitants shared with those who gathered, stored and cooked ingredients in their baskets. "We have to follow the old way, the traditional way," comments Julia Parker, who sat next to her daughter Lucy, "by repeating a continued consistent practice of weaving baskets." They experienced growing up in Yosemite Valley living with baskets and grinding rocks, as a part of their native identity, with tools having a variety of uses. "I could change this whole thing to make it modern, but to me it's more important knowing how they did it the old way and to keep that story going. Today, we can make food faster than those using modern conveniences; our way may look hard today, but it is quicker."

Circling youngsters surrounded the setting, running by gleefully. Julia sits down beside one of her woven baskets and explains their way of life. "In the village, ladies would have different jobs to help, and it takes a lot of effort. There would be different chores. Some were making baskets and the others entertaining the kids by telling stories and singing songs, like we do now. They would often cook only one meal in the morning, where everyone would get together. There, they ate a big meal, often berries could be gathered and it was so nice…and peaceful." Julia continues to tell her story while sitting and working the raw acorns into flour. "When the leaves yellow and the rain falls, that is when acorns are harvested." Julia then cracks one open. "In the seed of the acorn, when the acorn falls and the little 'hat' sticks on the acorn, some have an insect in it. See, that didn't make a very good sound. When they are a good acorn, see that snap, that's a good sound and you are going to get a good acorn. Then, see how all the skin comes off. And then when the skin comes off, we can turn it into flour." Checking with a small knife point, Julia continues to inspect the kernels in order to eliminate those with imperfections or damage. "We have to split that seed now. It has to be split, and we open it up like this. Then it is ready to pound."

Pow Wow in Bridgeport.

Julia has a small pounding stone and a tall stone mortar to which she adds the fresh kernel to already worked flour. This is where the real work of pounding out the acorn flour is done, inside what is typically called a grinding rock. "It all has to go in there clean, it can't have any of the red on it. The ladies will know, because they'll take a look at your flour, and if you have a lot of the red in it, then they can tell if you are lazy. They can also tell if you cracked this acorn wrong—the kernels will get all mashed up. You want to make it even," says Julia as she displays her acorn flour. "You see, when you prepare food you want it to look pretty and want to have it nice and clean…they were immaculate with a special brush for the flour and a special brush for scrubbing the baskets out. You have to crack it the way I crack it to make it look nice. That's how I was taught,"

The education of Native American culture continues with people like Julia in teaching the next generations.

she implores. "We always have a starter, just like sourdough, to keep it from getting oily, so it will be nice and fluffy, like flour. You see, if you keep pounding, this will turn to oil. These were last year's acorns and these acorns are six years old," as Julia reveals another basketful. "They keep indefinitely when in the shell. They'll last for ten, twelve, fifteen years; and the reason for the acorn lasting a long time, you see, is because in Yosemite Valley the acorn doesn't come every year." Julia continues to demonstrate the proper sitting position. "You're stretched out and you pound. I didn't bring my big fifteen to twenty pound rock that I lift up and bring down. It crushes it in no time. I always tell the young girls, if they want to learn how to pound acorn we do a one-hand rock and we do a five pound rock. Then, if you want to be a Jayne Mansfield, they work the twenty pound rock. Not many people sit on the ground and lift weights! The heavier the rock, the quicker you are going to get your flour. You are developing your hands, your arms are getting strong and you are getting yourself ready for when you do your basket. You need to have good strong hands," Julia explains, "in order to weave a basket." Soon, the acorn begins to make its transformation. "We need to pound, and you watch a few minutes, you'll see it will turn to flour. What's happening is that all the heavy kernels fall inside the center with the vibration," as she points to the center of the large mortar. "Then it is time to sift. I can put my hand in there and there is lots of fine flour on my hand. Now it is time to take out the powder." Julia and Lucy serve acorn hors d'oeuvres, "just enough to hold in your hand."

Julia Parker retells the story of Native American food gathering over the millennia used by California indigenous tribes.

Then, deer meat, berries, fish and insects are also served. "We eat the cacagee insect from Mono Lake, and the peeogee insect from trees around Mammoth. It's all sweet," says Julia, "and all protein; probably a 95% high protein diet!" Julia stresses that the grinding rocks are also a very important part of this process. "My rock is a special one-hand rock; this is for a woman, a young girl who is beginning to pound acorns. We give her a light rock. Then, you want to get your hands, your whole body set for this. You see, you are going to be working at it. The women were exceptionally strong, they were always cutting their willow and fixing their baskets; they were quite strong, their hands were incredibly strong. It's a life that can disappear with time, in a millennium," but who would think the Indians were carrying these traditions? "This is as close as we can get to our old ways, and this will always be the same because the rocks are here, and what is inside of every Native American will never die, because these people don't want to forget the traditional ways." Mother and daughter, Julia and Lucy Parker's baskets are found at museums and may be seen first hand at tribal gatherings near Yosemite, as well as nationally.

Lucy Parker, Julia's daughter displays the art of indigenous California, representing the sustenance gained from gathering native foods and native life existing over centuries. (Dan Barta)

Rafters along the American River's South Fork in Coloma.

GOLD RUSH HISTORIC PARKS

MARSHALL GOLD DISCOVERY STATE HISTORIC PARK

310 BACK STREET, COLOMA 530-622-3470

From Sacramento via US Highway 50 in Placerville, turn north on Highway 49 and follow the South Fork of the American River eight miles to Coloma at Sutter's Mill and the Gold Discovery site. The American River flows through Coloma Valley at the California State Historic Marshall Gold Discovery Park, the Discovery Museum, and the Marshall Monument, where the 'Gold Strike Heard Around The World' was recorded on January 24, 1848. This single Eureka! event became the center of world attention, and the first rumors of gold ignited an irresistible fervor after the discovery by James W. Marshall of two nuggets in the tail race at Sutter's Mill, at the river edge. The imposing sawmill stands high above the river and is a working replica of the original water-powered Sutter's Mill and a significant early California historical site. Try your luck at panning gold in the American River, or enjoy picnics and wildflower hikes crossing the river from the Mount Murphy Bridge. The mill site first built by Marshall was rediscovered during the 1940s a short distance upstream on the South Fork from the rebuilt sawmill. The old mining town historical buildings from the authentic past are built of wood, brick, and stone remain intact. Of the earliest, the schoolhouse is where American scholar, poet, and lecturer Edwin Markham had taught. John Studebaker began manufacture in 1853 at the buggy and wheelbarrow shop in Coloma, where living history events continue throughout the year. Buggy rides for viewing the park's 576 acres make a perfect day in the Gold Country for the entire family.

I. Sacramento Gold Country
Tour 1
Sacramento & El Dorado Counties
Sutter's Fort to Sutter's Mill

Thought to be the photo of James W. Marshall posed in front of the original Sutter's Mill, circa 1850.
(Library of Congress)

On a 35-mile scenic journey from Sacramento, take the path to the historic gold discovery site in Coloma at Sutter's Mill. In Placerville, Highway 49 and US Highway 50 converge near the river's edge, eight miles from Sutter's Mill and the Marshall Gold Discovery State Historic Park. James W. Marshall in January 1848 constructed a sawmill at the first gold discovery site. A worldwide migration followed into the California Gold Country and began the 1849 Gold Rush. Within 576 acres, the park presents living history events for visitors each season. A centerpiece of historic California, the small community of Coloma today consists of 20 authentic Gold Rush buildings on the riverfront with wildflower trails, and streets leading to a Gold Discovery Museum, a blacksmithing shop, churches, old schoolhouse, and its residents.

The native term Cullumah, or Beautiful Valley, described by the indigenous Nisenan language, defines the idyllic serenity surrounding the iconic river. After the discovery of two small nuggets, James W. Marshall was quoted to say, "My eye was caught with the glimpse of something shining in the ditch." John A. Sutter tested and confirmed the golden material while attempting to keep secret any suspicion of any presence of gold nuggets they found along the riverbed. Then, unavoidably, news of gold…Gold…GOLD! had spread nonetheless. A single spark ignited the largest-ever worldwide migration in history. The original Sutter's Fort grew into a town and renamed in honor of the Sacramento River by John Sutter's son and Sam Brannan.

Today, the experience in visiting Coloma steps into the incredible age of the Sierra Nevada foothill California Gold Rush, where one stands in the moment near the giant authentic full-scale working replica sawmill on the riverbank, and the place where fever-pitched prospectors began a golden era of tent camps in 1848. Guided walking tours retell the story before and after the gold discovery, repeated twice daily. In mid-October, from 10AM–4PM or on the

Sutter's Mill, at the site of the Gold Discovery.

first week in December, for Christmas in Coloma, join in the fun and reenactment of Gold Discovery Day. Admission to the event includes vehicle parking and visitors hear the lore of incredible forty-niner gold discoveries and discouragements, and enjoy living history events at the sprawling tent camps re-created throughout the park. At Gold Rush Live!, visitors register a claim at the Assay/Claims Office, procure supplies at the General Store, eat at the Boarding House, and find a place to bunk down. If you've just come in from the mines, there's time to venture over to the gambling hall, then head on over to the Barber and Bath House to clean up. Don't miss picking up a fresh shirt at the Laundry before heading to the saloon. When there's time, visit the doctor, a blacksmith, and surveyor in town. But remember to take all you hear with a grain of salt, as tall tales prevail with rumors flying.

Inside the Gold Discovery Museum, visitors find exhibits of mining equipment and elementary tools, horse-drawn carriages, and unusual historical memorabilia preserved from the area. Several films presented on history bring to light revealing techniques in finding gold. The nearby Marshall Monument Trail begins in the park and makes an overland round trip with a 1.5-mile loop and a 250-foot climb in elevation. Much to the delight of all, there's a spot for gold panning during park hours on the east side of the river, across the Mount Murphy Bridge. Choices

Sacramento Gold Country

The stone buildings in view of Sutter's Mill at Marshall Gold Discovery Park are known as the Wah Hop and Man Lee Stores built by Jonas Wilder before 1860, then leased to Chinese merchants.

Sparks fly at Marshall Gold Discovery State Historic Park at 'Living History' events on special weekends.

Gold Rush authentic living history events, and tent camps are presented annually at Gold Rush Live, each October.

GOLD RUSH CONTEMPORARY
JOHN AUGUSTUS SUTTER AT CENTER STAGE

John Augustus Sutter
(Library of Congress)

Arriving in 1839, to California's northern Sacramento River Valley, John A. Sutter would soon become the unsuspecting co-creator of the California Gold Rush of 1849. As a Mexican citizen, he had been awarded a land grant situated at the confluence of the American and Sacramento Rivers. His partnership with James W. Marshall propelled their ascendency into starring roles, initialized in the staging of Sutter's Mill, then making the first Gold Rush discovery in 1848. Afterwards, both men suffered a steep decline as their dreams of large holdings and rich rewards were dashed into thin air. Sutter's holdings spread all the way to the Pacific Ocean, yet provided little recourse from incursions made by the U.S. government. His claims in maintaining land holdings became a legal controversy cast to the courts decision. The final denial of all rights came to all Mexican Land Grant holders, with legislation aligned towards California's bid for U.S. Statehood in 1850. The law essentially left Sutter at the mercy of U.S. government for scant subsidies.

Sutter's customary habit to overextending his credit amassed large paper holdings, and subsequently, he never was able to reimburse the debts he incurred. As early as May 29, 1848, The San Francisco Californian reported, "The whole country, from San Francisco to Los Angeles, from the seashore to the base of the Sierra Nevada, resounded with the sordid cry of 'gold...Gold...GOLD' while fields were left half planted, the house half built, and everything neglected but the manufacture of shovels and pickaxes." In increasing numbers, the goldseekers passing through Sutter's Fort, as well the frequent squatters and random settlers, went well beyond his control. His reliance

Captain Sutter enjoyed appearing to guests in full military regalia.
(Mayo Hayes O'Donnell Library)

on friendships, investments, or paid labor using his cheerful habit giving gifts in patronizing appeasement, also disappeared. Several decades of early missionary malaria infestations had decimated California's native populations from 200,000 to a mere 20,000, and the Gold Rush further diminished the nations of indigenous Miwok, Nisenan, and other tribes. The events caused Sutter's reliances on outside labor supporting his enterprises, making them doubly impossible.

Sacramento Gold Country

Gold Rush tent camps with visitors at Sutters Mill Living History Events, on the American River.

of activities include panning for gold, wildflower trails, biking, hiking, river rafting, kayaking, and buggy rides. The park recommends bringing your pan or purchasing one at the Mercantile Shop. Interpretive exhibits and programs on gold discovery are presented daily and offer a prelude to making the journey along the Golden Chain on Highway 49.

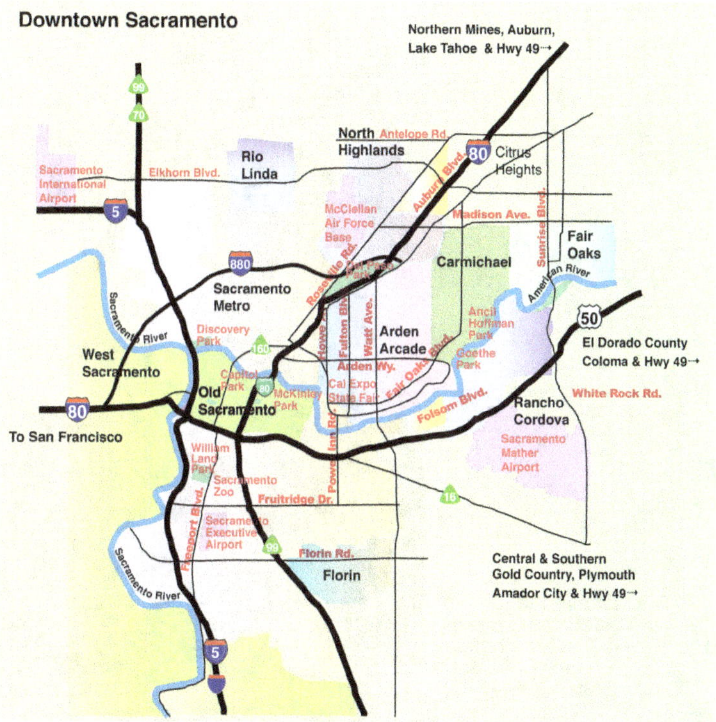

Downtown Sacramento

Frank Bekeart's Gunsmith Shop is one of the oldest buildings in town. Bekeart had built the brick building in 1855.

The Marshall Monument is located at the end of Highway 153, at the junction of Cold Springs Road and State Highway 49.

James W. Marshall was hired to construct a sawmill powered by the river current. The mill was rebuilt during the 1970s, designed as a working replica near the gold discovery site, on the American River's South Fork.

Visitors to Marshall State Historic Park enjoy unique opportunities to walk around the grounds, or hop on a carriage ride along Highway 49's pioneer pathway.

GOLD RUSH CONTEMPORARY
JAMES W. MARSHALL'S EXTRAORDINARY EUREKA!

James Marshall continued living near Sutter's Mill.

After meeting on a bend of the American River in August 1847, James W. Marshall and John Sutter began a partnership to build a lumber mill. In their agreement, according to Sutter, the ownership rights to the sawmill and land assets depended on each man's sworn citizenship. Since Marshall, a carpenter, was an American, then Sutter, at the time, a Mexican patriot, claimed full ownership while foreseeing California becoming an American territory would make their partnership equal after independence from Mexico. Well before Marshall started on the mill each man pilfered away their interests in the ownership, selling off pieces to investors. When the news first circulated by laborers witnessing the remarkable event made on January 24, 1848 inadvertently had alerted thousands, an initial local Gold Rush began as rumors flew widely about Marshall's gold discovery. Soon, a stampede of prospectors inundated the territory buying up gold claims staked at 20' x 25' or larger, all along the riverfront. Marshall became a celebrity in his role igniting the Gold Rush, and later, many became convinced of Marshall's mysterious talents of knowing where to find gold, and he proceeded to misguide a few dismayed gold seekers more often than not yielding any result.

By 1850, Marshall spent time in and around Coloma working in the carpentry trade. He and Sutter applied openly to the Governor and U.S. Congress to receive lifetime pensions, but with little result. By the 1860s, Marshall planted grapes as an attempt in winemaking, then found himself unable to compete against other vineyards. With the help of George Frederic Parsons, editor of the Sacramento Record, Marshall wrote his memoirs in 1870, then failed to sell many copies. Supported by neighbors, he lived a subsistence life to age 75. At the end of California's shortest highway, State Highway 153, one mile from downtown Coloma, an honorary Marshall Monument stands over 41-feet tall, with his likeness portrayed in a golden bronze statue pointing to the direction of the river bank where he discovered gold at Sutter's Mill.

TOUR 2
SACRAMENTO COUNTY

View from Firehouse Alley in Old Sacramento at sundown.

OLD SACRAMENTO WALKING TOUR

The City of Sacramento includes many vintage Gold Rush sites in history, and at mid-town begins with Sutter's Fort State Historic Park and the State Indian Museum. Pedestrians walk along L Steet for 12 blocks to the State Capitol Mall's expansive memorial garden grounds and museum. From there, a short walk to the K Street Shopping Mall leads to a tour in Old Sacramento, approached through a convenient tunnel inside the parking garage under the I-5 Freeway on J Street, adjacent to 2nd Street. A centerpiece of the Gold Rush, the once bustling streets in Old Sacramento are in view of 53 early brick structures within six blocks of downtown cobblestone streets. Visit shops, restaurants, boardwalks, and a walk to the riverfront edge where Firehouse Alley, a narrow path dividing the entire length of the Old Sacramento State Historic Park, leads towards the railyard and California State Railroad Museum and Library. Next door, the 1855 Big Four Building stands in a line of the venerable brick structures, once housing the Huntington & Hopkins Hardware Store and the historical western station terminus of the Pony Express in 1860. In 1853, the B.F. Hastings Building was a home to the early California Supreme Court. At the confluence of the American and Sacramento River from 1849, the Eagle Theatre, California's original performances gave the forty-niners evenings of entertainment along the riverbank. The Jedidiah Strong Smith American River Memorial Biking and Walking Trail honors the American explorer and fur trapper, who traveled here between 1827-1828. The awe-inspiring bike path beginning in Discovery Park follows the banks of the American River east over 23 miles, all the way to Old Folsom.

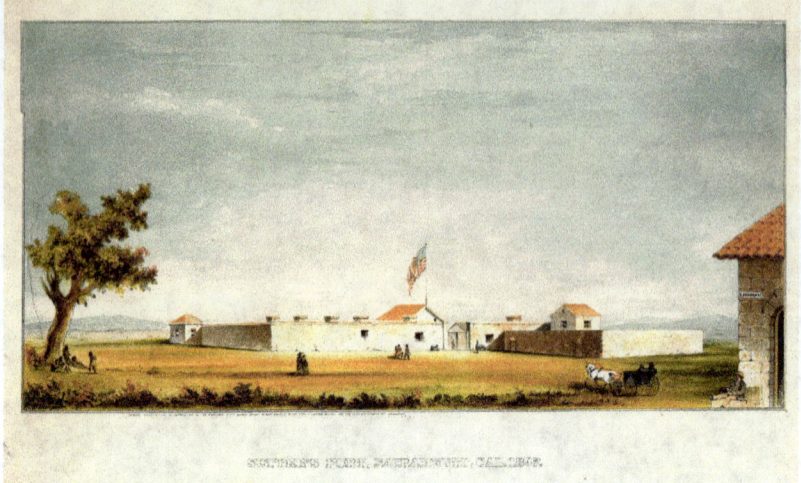

A portrait of 'Sutter's Fort 1847' was handed down in the 1860s to the US Government Archives with an inscription by Sam Brannan. (Library of Congress)

Although you wouldn't expect it, the brick basements in Old Sacramento at one time were the first floors of the very earliest brick buildings. The waterfront banks often flooded due to the incessant deluge of the rainy season, with the tide waters of the Sacramento River rising into the streets. In the 1860s and 1870s, the town decided to raise the street level up a single story higher above the original streets from 1849, making the buildings first stories into the basement foundations, then adding second stories at the new street level and rebuilding the entire town at the higher ground level.

SUTTER'S FORT CALIFORNIA STATE PARK
2701 L STREET, SACRAMENTO, CA 916-445-4422
Visit the grounds of the original Sutter's Fort located between 26th and 28th, and K and L Streets, in Sacramento, with its fascinating collection of early California items. Both guided and self-guided tours on the grounds. The State Indian Museum is directly across from the fort on K Street.

CALIFORNIA STATE INDIAN MUSEUM
2618 K STREET 916-324-0971
The State Indian Museum next to Sutter's Fort offers a fascinating glimpse into California's history and illustrates culture, arts, and lifestyles of our State's diverse culture of its indigenous population. Self-guided tours provide opportunities to celebrate the heritage of California Indian culture from the traditions of ancestral to contemporary generations. Special events include Ishi Day, Acorn Day, Gathering of Honored Elders, and exhibit a showcase discussing the effect of the Gold Rush. Daily 10AM – 5PM, Admission Fee.

Steam locomotive tours in Old Sacramento at the Front Street depot.

CALIFORNIA STATE CAPITOL MUSEUM
1315 10TH STREET AT L STREET, STATE CAPITOL ROOM B-27 916-324-0333

The Capitol Park Memorial Grounds are in memory of Civil War soliders and was planted in 1896 with trees from several important battlefields. Its a labyrinth of 12-blocks with gardens, statues, and browsing areas surrounding the California State Capitol, and just seven city-blocks east of Old Sacramento and Front Street riverbank shops and museums. The State Capitol is a depository of many important historical documents, iconic paintings, and Gold Rush artifacts. The State Capitol is a working State House and State Park Museum open to the public for exploring the past, present, and future of State government. Guided Capitol Park tours occur Memorial Day through Labor Day. M-F, 7:30AM–6PM Weekends, 9AM–5PM, Free Admission.

CALIFORNIA STATE LIBRARY
914 CAPITOL MALL 916-323-9843

Founded in 1850, located across the street from the State Capitol in the heart of downtown Sacramento, the neoclassical Stanley Mosk Library and Courts Building is listed on the National Register of Historic Places. The library stores over 5 million items. Weekdays 9:30AM-4PM, Free Admission.

CALIFORNIA STATE RAILROAD MUSEUM
2ND AND I STREETS 916-445-6645

Look for steam train rides during weekends, April-September. Board a million-pound steam locomotive, step into a Pullman sleeping car, examine the beautiful dining car china and other treasures. A Smithsonian Affiliate, the State Railroad Museum at Old Sacramento State Historic Park is the largest of its kind in the West. It's known for highlighting transcontinental exhibits and several eras of western railroads. Daily 10AM – 5PM, Admission Fee.

The original earliest landmark, Sutter's Fort greets visitors to an authentic setting of California's past. Here, American settlers organized the Bear Flag Revolt of 1846.

SACRAMENTO HISTORY MUSEUM
101 I STREET 916-808-7059
Formerly the Discovery Museum History Center, the Sacramento History Museum is a true celebration of all aspects of life in Sacramento over the past 200 years. The Museum tells the stories of our city founders, rivers, the Gold Rush, agriculture, the media, industry, culture and more. If it happened in Sacramento, it's happening at the Sacramento History Museum. Tues–Sat. 11AM–4PM, Free Admission.

D.O. MILLS BANK BUILDING
226 J STREET
First erected in 1852 on J Street west of 3rd Street. It was moved in 1864 to 226 J Street. The D.O. Mills Bank was one of the oldest and largest banks of early California in 1849, and first on the Pacific Coast. Mills became the president of the San Francisco Bank of California in 1864.

B.F. HASTINGS BUILDING
2ND & J STREET
The site of B.F. Hastings Bank built in 1850, also was occupied by Wells Fargo & Co., and the offices of the Sacramento Valley Railroad, and the Alta Telegraph Co. Between April, 1860–May, 1861, Alta Telegraph, and its successor, The California State Telegraph Co., were agents for the Central Overland Pony Express. Its first departure began eastward from this site on April 4, 1860.

Old Sacramento's riverfront depot at the terminus of the transcontinental railroad and a center of tourism.

CALIFORNIA AUTOMOBILE MUSEUM
2200 FRONT STREET 916-442-6802
Experience automotive evolution at the California Automobile Museum. From the invention of the car and into the future, the exhibits include modern and classic vehicles from all over the world. Enjoy a tour by a knowledgeable docent. Weds–Mon 10AM–5PM. Closed Tuesday.

OLD SACRAMENTO SCHOOLHOUSE MUSEUM
1200 FRONT STREET 916-483-8818
The yellow Old Sacramento Schoolhouse allows you to experience California's early days of education in a living replica of an 1800s one-room schoolhouse. Enjoy the photographs, books, pot-bellied stove, desks, rose garden and playground with other antique items from the Gold Rush era, but be on your best behavior, or the schoolmarm might make you stay late and clap the dust off the erasers. Mon–Sat 10AM–4PM; Sun 1–4PM, Free Admission.

CALIFORNIA MUSEUM ARCHIVES PLAZA
1020 O STREET 916-653-7524
One block south of the State Capitol, home of the official California Hall of Fame, "California Museum educates, enlightens and inspires visitors on California's rich history and legacy of influence on the world through ideas, innovation, the arts and culture. Through interactive and innovative exhibits and programming, the Museum inspires men, women and children to dream the California dream and to make their own mark on history." Formerly the Golden State Museum telling the story of our great state, the museum promotes California's artistic and cultural heritage and provides a home for the stories of California's women. The Museum offers family guides, educational materials, discounted group rates, and a California specialty gift shop. Tues–Sat 10AM–5PM; Sun 12–5PM, Admission Fee.

The Delta King, a 285-foot paddlewheel riverboat permanently docked in on the Sacramento River waterfront, in Old Sacramento.

SACRAMENTO CITY CEMETERY
BROADWAY AT 10TH STREET 916-448-0811

An outdoor museum, the cemetery is adorned with ornate statues, dramatic markers and lush gardens providing an important record of California history from the Gold Rush Era, through modern times. Keep an eye out for the popular 'Lantern Tours' held in October. Established in 1850, it includes grave sites of cholera victims from that year; as well as illustrious citizens including California Governor John Bigler, Newton Booth, and William Irwin. Also, George Wright, hero of the Mexican War; Mark Hopkins, builder of the Central Railroad; Hardin Bigelow, first Sacramento Mayor; William S. Hamilton, son of Alexander Hamilton; E.B. Crocker, Associate Justice of the California Supreme Court, founder of the Crocker Art Museum, and counsel to the Big Four which included his younger brother, Charles Crocker, of the Central Pacific Railroad and First Transcontinental Railroad, are all interred here. Free Admission.

SOJOURNER TRUTH AFRICAN AMERICAN MUSEUM
2251 FLORIN ROAD 916-320-9573

Named in honor of the celebrated abolitionist and women's rights activist, the Sojourner Truth Multicultural Arts Museum is dedicated to bringing African, Asian, Hispanic and Native American art to the general public. Displays of art from around the world, the museum features an extensive list of workshops, classes and special events. Mon–Fri 8AM–4 PM; Sat–Sun 10AM–5:30PM, by appointment.

Sacramento Gold Country

The New Ship "MECHANICS' OWN" built for the Mechanics' Mining Association by Messrs. Bishop & Simonson, Sailed from New York, Aug! 14th 1849, for California.
Published & for Sale at 136 Chatham Street.

Tall ships were commonplace transportation bringing travelers joining the Gold Rush as this stately Mining Association ship had in 1849. (Library of Congress).

OLD SACRAMENTO WATERFRONT

During the heyday of 1849 Gold Rush, Old Sacramento was at the center of commerce on the edge of the Sacramento River waterfront. The Delta King paddlewheeler is permanently moored there at 1000 Front Street, and its historic twin sister, the Delta Queen, were each built during the late 1920s Prohibition Era and transported passengers drinking and gambling on 10-hour cruises to San Francisco. The Delta King serves guests today with a full service restaurant, bar and grill, theater, and offers catering in the boat's Pilothouse for large parties. The hotel features forty-four AAA 3-Diamond-rated staterooms, each with riverfront views.

The 1861 Crocker Museum with its current 21st Century additional galleries, curates rare collections of modern local art and features fine original Gold Country oils.

CROCKER ART MUSEUM
216 O ST 916-808-7000

Judge Edwin B. and Margaret Crocker commissioned the construction of a Victorian-Italianate building to serve as a gallery for their art collection, in 1869. The museum is the oldest west of the Mississippi and built a year before the founding of the Metropolitan Museum of Art, the Boston Museum of Fine Art, and a decade before the founding the Art Institute of Chicago. On October 10, 2010, the grand opening of the Teel Family Pavilion tripled the Museum's size and added an educational, art studio, and resource center space for participatory arts for children and adults. It also has an expanded library and new student exhibition space. The Anne and Malcolm McHenry Works on Paper Study Center greatly improves access for visiting scholars and students studying the Crocker's outstanding master drawings collection. To celebrate the 100th birthday of Sacramento's most renowned artist, the Crocker Art Museum presented Wayne Thiebaud 100: Paintings, Prints, and Drawings, in 2020. Best known for his tantalizing paintings of cakes and pies, Thiebaud has long been affiliated with Pop Art, though his body of work is far more expansive. Newer amenities at the gallery include a 260-seat auditorium, a café with indoor and outdoor seating, and a redesigned Crocker Art Museum Store. The first floor is open to the public free of charge with free Wi-Fi available. Fri–Weds. 10AM–5PM, Thurs. 10AM-9PM Admission fee at main museum.

GOVERNOR'S MANSION STATE HISTORIC PARK
16TH AND H STREET

Built in 1877, the Governor's Mansion is a regal Victorian mansion that was the home of California's governors from George Pardee in 1903 until Ronald Reagan took office in the late 1960s. While the Capitol acted as the office, this mansion acted as the family home. Opulently decorated rooms have tales, secrets and mischief of the families that lived there. The Governor's Mansion State Historic Park remains temporarily closed to the public for repairs, until further notice.

Governor's Mansion State Historic Park remains closed for renovation.

LELAND STANFORD MANSION STATE HISTORIC PARK
800 N. STREET 916-324-0575

Leland Stanford served as California's governor for 13 years.

The Stanford home, two blocks from the State Capitol building, served as the state executive office from 1861 to 1867, before the Capitol building's completion. Constructed in 1860, the home of 'Big Four' member Leland Stanford, who was the governor of California from 1861-1874. It has 17-foot ceilings, gilded mirrors, carved moldings, elegant 19th century crystal and bronze light fixtures, historical paintings, and original period furnishings. The property is listed in the National Register and is now a State Park museum open to the public. Leland Stanford was a railroad tycoon and founder of Stanford University, purchasing what would become this elegant mansion for $8,000 in 1861. The four-story, 19,000 square foot Leland Stanford Mansion has a special historical and architectural significance. It served as the office of three early California governors, Leland Stanford, Fredrick Low and Henry Haight. Today, it serves as the State's official address for diplomatic and business receptions, as well as offering guided public tours. Guided half-hour tours daily, 10AM–5PM Admission Fee.

Museum of Medical History
5380 Elvas Ave. 916-456-3152
Experience the evolution of medicine from the Gold Rush to today in a unique museum presented by the Sierra Sacramento Valley Medical Society. Exhibits include an iron lung, patent medicines and pharmacology, Asian medicine, nursing, radiology, quackery and plenty that will make you grateful for today's modern medicine. Mon–Fri 9AM–4 PM; Closed holidays, Free admission.

Powerhouse Science Center
3615 Auburn Blvd. Sacramento 916-674-5000
A science center operated by the Sacramento Utility District bringing STEAM (science, technology, engineering, art and math) experiences to life for Sacramento and surrounding communities. Learn about natural, physical, and biological sciences through changing exhibitions. Weekends programs, activities, and planetarium shows. Special group/field trip programs including Challenger Learning Center missions. Hosted event space rental. Tues–Fri 12–4:30PM; Sat–Sun 10AM–4:30PM.

Mosac – Museum of Science and Curiosity
400 Jibboom St. Sacramento 916-674-5000
Sacramento's newest science museum is located in the historic power station overlooking Matsui WaterFront Park along the Sacramento River. A dynamic epicenter for STEAM education and an anchor point at Sacramento's waterfront. Science, Technology, Engineering, Art and Math.

Verge Center for the Arts
625 S Street 916-448-2985
Founded in 2008, Verge Center for the Arts is a nonprofit arts organization focused on the promotion and support of contemporary art in the Sacramento region. In addition to on-site artist studios, the center offers expansive gallery space, community education and a one-of-a-kind printmaking lab. Thurs-Sat 11AM–6PM; Sun 12–5PM. Closed Mondays and Tuesdays.

California Statewide Museum Collections Center
4940 Lang Ave., McClellan Air Base 916-263-0805
A State Park steward of historical collections developed over the past 130 years. The Museum preserves and explores the origins and breadth of State Parks Collections and cultural resources held in trust for the people of California. Tues 1-4PM, Free Admission.

Aerospace Museum of California
3200 Freedom Park Dr., McClellan
916-643-3192
Sit in the cockpit of an airplane and learn the stories of aircraft first hand, or explore the wonders of space. The Museum is a place where dreams take flight. Self-guided tours, Thurs-Sun 9AM–4PM.

Old Sacramento wagon and buggy rides are a traditional favorite for visitors arriving in old town.

FOLSOM HISTORY MUSEUM
823 SUTTER STREET, FOLSOM 916-985-2707
The Folsom History Museum houses a variety of artifacts chronicling the settlement and development of the Folsom area. The museum Native Americans, gold in California, the formation of mining camps, and ethnic groups who contributed to this area. Guests are encouraged to try their luck at a gold panning demonstration, examine artifacts from the old days and observe early Pioneer tools, Tues-Sun 11AM–4PM.

CALIFORNIA AGRICULTURE MUSEUM
1962 HAYS LANE, WOODLAND 530-666-9700
From downtown Sacramento, the California Agriculture Museum is the world's largest, and home of the Heidrick Tractor Collection & Event Center showcasing the marvels of agriculture and commercial trucking with 130,000 square feet of interactive one-of-a-kind exhibits, collection of antique agricultural equipment, Wed-Sat 10AM–4PM.

DON & JUNE SALVATORI PHARMACY MUSEUM
4030 LENNANE DRIVE, NATOMAS
916-779-1410 X326
Inspired by California's unique and rich history of pharmacy, the Don & June Salvatori California Pharmacy Museum is just what the doctor ordered. Celebrate the role of the pharmacist in promoting health and well-being since the state's inception in 1850. Mon-Fri by appointment, Free Admission.

LOCKE BOARDING HOUSE MUSEUM STATE HISTORIC PARK
13916 MAIN ST., WALNUT GROVE 916-776-1661

The Boarding House was built in 1909 where the workers of the Southern Pacific Railroad lived. In 2008, it became the Locke Boarding House, with exhibits and research facilities on the Sacramento River Delta. The exhibit serves as the information center for Locke, a charming historic Chinese Town. It is the only one built for the Chinese by the Chinese in the country. It is listed in the National Register of Historic Places by the National Park Service. Tues & Fri 12–4PM; Sat & Sun 11AM–3PM, Free Admission.

SACRAMENTO CHILDREN'S MUSEUM
2701 PROSPECT PARK DRIVE
SUITE 120, RANCHO CORDOVA 916-730-5079

The Sacramento Children's Museum in City Hall designed for children, eight and younger, features "learn-by-doing!" Explore, create and inspire. The museum includes hands-on exhibits featuring art, water, airways and raceways, and fun activities. There is also a special area for infants and toddlers to enjoy safe exploration. Members: Free. General Admission: Seniors and Military Members. Weds–Fri, 9-10:30AM, 11AM-12:30PM.

SACRAMENTO ZOO
3930 W. LAND PARK DRIVE 916-808-5888

At the Sacramento Zoo, "we are also proud to inspire appreciation, understanding, and respect for all living things through stimulating educational opportunities, wholesome recreation, and compassionate and innovative animal care." From train rides to giraffe encounters, wildlife stage shows to events, private rentals and world-class education programs and veterinary care, the zoo truly offers something for everyone. Feb-Oct. Hours: 9AM–5PM with last admission at 4PM, Nov-Jan 10AM –5PM, with last admission at 4PM, Admission Fee.

There are over 50 historical buildings in Old Sacramento from the mid-1800s within the 296-acre State Historic Park.

ROSEVILLE UTILITY EXPLORATION CENTER
1501 PLEASANT GROVE BLVD., ROSEVILLE
916-746-1550
The Roseville Utility Exploration Center is a one-of-a-kind learning center focused on inspiring stewardship of resources in everyday life. The Center teaches energy conservation, waste reduction, water-use efficiency, recycled water, watershed protection and wastewater management in a fun and engaging way. While you're here, explore our hands-on exhibit hall, pick up a free Planet Protector comic book, participate in a green living workshop and join us at one of our community events. 10AM–5PM Monday through Thursday and Saturday, closed Fridays and Sundays, Free Admission.

MAIDU MUSEUM & HISTORIC SITE
1970 JOHNSON RANCH DR., ROSEVILLE
916-774-5934
The museum is located at an ancient site where Nisenan Maidu families lived for 3,000 years. Walk the trail to see hundreds of bedrock mortars, deeply carved ancient petroglyph, native plants and animals. The museum presents interactive exhibits and displays, the outside trail wanders among the sprawling oaks the inhabitants depended on. Friday–Saturday 9AM–2PM, general admission fee. Free entry for under age 5, Tribal members, Military, Museum members.

Pony Express Monument on 2nd Street, Old Sacramento.

SACRAMENTO LANDMARKS

SUTTERVILLE
The first town site of 1844 laid out by John A. Sutter is two miles south on the riverfront, on higher ground near the flooding river bank. With Lansford W. Hastings and John Bidwell, Sutter built the original homes including George Zins, and the first brick building of 1847 in the region. The Sutterville Post Office operated between 1855-60.

EAGLE THEATRE
921 FRONT ST., OLD SACRAMENTO
The site of the first theater building in California of 1849, reconstructed in 1974.

NEW HELVETICA CEMETERY
ALHAMBRA, I & J STREETS
The first area cemetery established by Capt. John A. Sutter, in 1849.

FIRST STAGE COACH AND RAILROADING SITE FRONT & K STREET
The first site of the stage coach terminal of the 1850s, and Sacramento Valley Railroad of 1855.

In Sacramento, the 1922 Julia Morgan House is a designer's masterpiece estate and built during her time as the distinguished architect of the Hearst Castle.

HOME SITE OF NEWTON BOOTH
1015-17 FRONT ST., OLD SACRAMENTO
The store and home of Newton Booth, Governor of California between 1871-1873, and U.S. Senator 1873-1879.

THE ORLEANS HOTEL SITE
1018 2ND STREET, OLD SACRAMENTO
The Orleans Hotel was built in 1852 and served as a depot for stage companies.

SAM BRANNAN HOUSE SITE
112 J STREET, SACRAMENTO
Erected in 1853, on land owned by Sam Brannan, California's first millionaire. He used the location as a meeting place for the Pioneer Association and other organizations of the day. Brannan converted to Mormonism in 1842, famously in the first months of 1848 paraded along San Francisco's streets shouting, "gold, Gold, GOLD! on the American River!" waving a vial of gold.

Downtown Old Sacramento

Walking tours at the Sacramento waterfront in Old Sacramento include river tours to see the landmarks, including the iconic Tower Bridge in the background.

SACRAMENTO RIVER CRUISES
Climb aboard a touring ship and cruise the Sacramento River to celebrate the Gold Rush in Old Sacramento. Aboard the Capitol Hornblower you will enjoy a 1-hour river cruise, receive fun coloring sheets for kids, with a true narration of the Gold Rush and the historic river ways. There are multiple cruises leaving each day so choose the day and time that works best for your friends and family river trips. 1206 Front St., 279-205-3214.

MORMON ISLAND
By 1853, a full-scale mining town with over 2,500 inhabitants built a tent camp on the river bar until a fire swept through the town, and the island later abandoned was inundated during the completion of Folsom Dam in 1956.

TOUR 3
VIA US 50 EAST
SACRAMENTO TO OLD FOLSOM

Old Town Folsom's Sutter Street boardwalk meanders along vintage brick building era streets with speciality shops and restaurants.

OLD FOLSOM

In 1847, at the confluence of the North and South Forks of the American River, a West Point graduate and original founder of the area, Captain J. L. Folsom began building the town on the American River called Granite City. Early Spring of 1848, several Mormon Battalion soliders uncovered the second greatest California gold discovery on the North Fork of the American River at Mormon Island, 21 miles downstream from Sutter's Mill. The population in the area instantly increased into the thousands with the search for placer gold. Although the island was innundated below Folsom Lake later, the small mining town of old Folsom remains the center of several signficant gold mines. Upon the death of its founder in July, 1855, the town name became Folsom in his honor. Captain Folsom hired Theodore Judah to engineer the contruction of the Sacramento Valley Railroad and on February 12th, 1855, operational as the first western railroad and connected California's burgeoning mining industries to Sacramento's harbor. By 1869, Judah succeeded opening the high Sierra pass through Truckee, merging the western transcontinental railroad system to all rail systems, nationally celebrated with a Golden Spike at Promontory Summit in Utah. Today, Folsom is an idyllic recreational spot enjoyed by kayakers, hikers, and bikers along the winding 23-mile American River Bike Trail, from Folsom Lake to Discovery Park and the Sacramento River waterfront.

The Sacramento Valley Railroad and roundtable in downtown Old Folsom is a fifty-six foot long "A" frame or gallows-style table.

The completed Sacramento Valley Railroad opened its Folsom depot in 1856 and established stops to Sacramento Valley 14 years before the transcontinental railroad arrived in California. The SVRR returned trains towards Sacramento from the revolving forty-foot turntable supported at ground level, now recreated in downtown Old Folsom. During the mining era, the developmental use of mechanical bucket-line dredging began in 1898 had spread throughout the Gold Country, swallowing up water and gravel aggregate from the river's bottom. Gravel was processed at the stamp mills, then sluiced with chemical preparations for the removal of the gold. Along the banks of the American River, more than one billion cubic yards of gravel was dredged by the Natomas Company to equal a profitable output of $125,000,000. Dredging was carried out through the 1950s leaving mere cobblestones with some noticeable remnants visible along US Highway 50.

Folsom Museums

Folsom History Museum
823 Sutter Street, Folsom 916-985-2707

The Folsom History Museum houses permanent exhibits chronicling the settlement and development of the Folsom area. Learn about native peoples, its pioneer settlers of the Gold Rush, railroad, agriculture and businesses. Group tours are available. Novel gift shop items offering visitors gifts. Oct–July, Wed-Sun 11AM – 4PM; Daily Aug–Sept. Nominal Admission Fee.

The Square Outdoor Museum – Makerspace
196 Wool Street, Folsom 916-801-2530

Pioneer Village is an outdoor living history museum and interactive interpretive area, including gold panning and a working blacksmith forge. Explore a miner's cabin, Southern Pacific Railroad caboose, and walk through the historical Ashland Station. Open Fri–Sun, 10AM to 3PM.

A testament to the 'Chinese Wall' laborers of 1869, and the landmark Sierra Tunnel Snow Sheds visible from I-80, a last step in building the transcontinental railroad lines.

THE FOLSOM POWERHOUSE STATE HISTORIC PARK
916-985-4843

The 1850 Folsom Powerhouse introduced innovative 20th Century technology for generating power. Horatio Gates Livermore pioneered the development of ditches and dams on the American River to serving industry and agriculture. Livermore's sons moving ahead, constructed the new powerhouse in Folsom and established the Natoma Water and Mining Company. By 1895, a momentous advance was implemented in generating and transmitting electricity in sending power to Sacramento City, downstream 23 miles away. The facility was the first to transmit high-voltage alternating current over long distance electric lines. The basic equipment continued operations until the hydroelectric plant was shut down in 1952. Group tours may be arranged to see the massive General Electric transformers in addition with the canal water system from the Folsom Dam.

The Old Folsom Powerhouse.

GOLD RUSH CONTEMPORARY
SAMUEL H. BRANNAN
CALIFORNIA'S FIRST MILLIONAIRE

Sam Brannan sold hardware to the migrants on their way to the Sierra Nevada goldfields.

California's first millionaire, Samuel Brannan was an ubiquitous figure and a larger-than-life storefront merchandiser seen nearly everywhere throughout the early days of the Gold Rush. He became a one-third owner in the second gold discovery site early in 1848 named Mormon Island, on the American River North Fork near Old Folsom. He was a designated bishop of the Mormon Church and helped church members back east to evacuate, and in 1846 led them to San Francisco's original settlement of Yerba Buena. Also, Brannan was an industrious journalist, newspaper publisher, supplier of goods, energetic entrepreneur, and highly regarded businessman. He brought with him a printing press in 1847 and founded the first San Francisco newspaper, the California Star. He promoted the Gold Rush up and down the city streets of San Francisco after investing in supply goods to sell the flurries of miners striking out into the Foothills. He owned multiple stores, opening one inside Sutter's Fort, one in San Francisco, and another in Coloma, serving the initial waves of miners on their way to the Sierra goldfields.

Brannan bought two square miles of land from John Sutter near Nicolaus on the Feather River. He built a story-and-a-half dwelling with an imposing winding stairway and eight rooms, each with a fireplace. In 1853, he was elected to the California State Senate. Brannan invested in Napa County's northern valley, and after mixing the names California and Saratoga, created Calistoga Springs building a vineyard, hotel, and resort with 20 cottages. By 1858, he planted the hillsides with plentiful harvests of superior wine and table grapes. As a project in support of Mormon unity, he established a village called New Hope, in the northern San Joaquin Valley at the mouth of the Stanislaus River. Renaming the town Stanislaus City, the river's surge destroyed it, and he moved the entire downtown to the opposite side to avoid flooding, renaming it San Joaquin City. Brannan designed the town to prosper over several decades and lined with hotels, saloons, and homes, then disbanded and quickly vanished. During the later years of his life, Sam Brannan through divorce and debts lost his holdings and moved to Mexico. He returned to San Francisco paying off all debtors settling near San Diego in Escondido in 1889 nearly penniless, he lived to the age of 70.

The downtown Old Folsom mural portrays the early years of California's Gold Rush, displayed at the corner of Sutter St.

FOLSOM PRISON MUSEUM
312 3RD STREET, FOLSOM 916-985-2707
Prison artifacts and Johnny Cash memorabilia fill the small museum and gift shop, located near Old Town in a vintage home.

ZITTEL FAMILY AMPHITHEATER
200 WOOL ST., HISTORIC FOLSOM DISTRICT
Near the American River and Lake Natoma, relaxed seating for events of Shakespeare, concerts, plays and civic ceremonies is located behind the Historic Folsom Railroad Depot Information Center. Parking is available at 905 Leidesdorff Street. Free Admission.

CONSUMNES RIVER MINING CAMPS
A sizable encampment of miners gathered on the Consumnes River at the southeast line of Sacramento at Michigan Bar with placer mining operations had an increased population with over 1,500. Decades later, the entire town was swept away from upstream hydraulic mining.

SLOUGH HOUSE
Roads to the southern mines passed over the Consumnes River requiring ferries and toll bridges at an early date. Jared Sheldon, co-owner of Omochumnes Mexican grant completed Slough House in 1850 on the Deer Creek tributary of Consumnes River along State Highway 16 and Jackson–Sacramento Road. Near there, other fleeting towns had a little future; such as Cook's Bar, founded by Dennis Cook in 1849, vanished ten years later. Five miles southwest on Ione Valley Road, Sebastopol, named during the Crimean War was a lively camp between 1854 to 1859. Also, Katesville's town site offered a hotel with several stores and saloons, and deserted by 1862.

TOUR 4
EL DORADO COUNTY VIA US 50
SACRAMENTO TO PLACERVILLE

ON THE GOLDEN CHAIN OF HIGHWAY 49'S GOLD RUSH MINING TOWNS

Placerville's town fire alarm is a cast bell shipped in 1865 from England. The old 50-foot wooden tower supports were replaced with steel in 1898.

DOWNTOWN PLACERVILLE

The Emigrant Trail led pioneers along the path of today's US Highway 50 to the 1849 Gold Rush with explorers and prospectors crossing the Sierra Mountain Range at the 8,600-foot elevation. A new trail south of Lake Tahoe opened by wagons, stagecoaches, and mule trains cut through El Dorado National Forest near the Desolation Wilderness and became California's first US Highway in 1895. Passing over the mountainous terrain at Carson Pass, unlike the Truckee route with over 27 rivers, an improved southern crossing ascended two summits and forded three rivers on the way towards Placerville. The route was surveyed in 1852 as the shortest low-elevation trail for emigrants entering the goldfields on the American River. In 1848, a tent camp was set up on high ground by Sutter's men at Weber Creek named Old Dry Diggings, and a placer mining settlement known for its limited water resources 10 miles from Sutter's Mill in Coloma. The new destination acquired the name Hangtown after developing an unsavory reputation reported in the newspapers that carried eerie stories about hanging notorious desparatos and thieves with descriptions of the old hang tree at Elstner's Hay Yard downtown, now a California Historical Landmark at 305 Main Street. After rich gold deposits at Hangtown Creek and Cedar Ravine were discovered in 1848, 50 log cabins inhabited the area

Sacramento Gold Country

The Placerville City Hall, 3101 Center Street.

with more than 40 original Gold Rush buildings established in and around Main Street. Several fires from 1856 and later were a part of the town's history. In 1854, the town was renamed Placerville and began to grow when miners redirected water resources from higher elevations to reach the surface mines where placer aggregate gold was dug out, washed, and separated using sluices yielding lucrative mineral ore. Old Hangtown was the earliest most frequented Gold Rush destination along Highway 50, as destinations were settled along the way between Apple Hill, Camino, Kyburz, Strawberry, Twin Bridges, Meyers, and Lake Tahoe. Scenic drives in El Dorado County and Placerville also follow the old Pony Express Trail to make stops at the Nevada House in Coloma, between April 3, 1860 and October 26, 1861. A settler from Norway at Putah Creek near Placerville, John A. "Snowshoe" Thompson, famously traversed the Sierra snows on long wooden skis during the long Sierra winters of 1856-76, hauling 60 to 80 pounds of mail sledding back and forth to Genoa, Nevada. Today, eight miles from Coloma, downtown Placerville is a thriving Gold Country community with nearly 90 historical buildings and homes.

There are galleries, shops, restaurants, lodging, and ranches with orchards and vineyards surrounding it. Main Street has many buildings of historical significance, in itself making an edifying walking tour. Built as a hub on the Old Lincoln Highway from Sacramento, US 50 begins the trek across the continent on its way east. California's third largest Gold Rush town was named Placerville in 1854, and became the county seat in 1857. City Hall was established in 1860 at 487-489 Main Street. The Old Town Centre and Masonic Hall from 1893 are located at 413-423 Main Street. The Snowshoe Thompson Statue stands at Sacramento & Main Streets and the Old West Trading Post at 320 Main Street. Two significant historical homes in Placerville are the Chichester-McKee House from 1892, and the 1895 Combellack Blair House.

Placerville Hardware welcomes visitors to the oldest hardware store in the West.

John Mohler Studebaker, transportation expert arrived setting up shop in Placerville and Coloma during the early 1850s. He was one of five brothers in the wagon-making trade, and the family founder of the Studebaker Corporation. The location of his blacksmith shop at California Historical Landmark at 543 Main Street, he made wagon wheels and sold handmade wheelbarrows for $10 to the 49ers where he amassed a fortune of $8,000 and acquired the nickname "Wheelbarrow Johnny". He later returned home to join his brothers' carriage-making factory in South Bend, Indiana and by 1901, John was the last surviving family member with his son-in-law Fred Fish, when the company considered electric cars at the time as their main product. Studebaker acquired many partnerships and emerged as the Studebaker Company in 1911, at the time producing only gas-powered vehicles. From 1868 to 1917, John Studebaker was an honorary company president until age 83, the year he passed away.

From the earliest days, placer mining became a lucrative source of finding gold either by panning, sluicing, or digging out the surface ledges, as increasingly laborious methods had become necessary in driving mining shafts deeper and deeper. "Hydrauliking" and its powerful monitor cannons with volumes of high pressure water washed gravel and aggregate from ancient river beds, canyons, and hills, at productive areas near Placerville. Nearly $25,000,000 was sifted out from the old placer mines using hydraulic output. One mile south of Placerville at Coon Hollow, large amounts of placer finds were sluiced making $10,000,000 in yields, between 1861 and 1871. Surface mining and use of water cannons at Little Spanish Hill, just south of Placerville at Big Spanish Hill, generated $6,000,000 in high-grade ore. At Smith's Flat, east of Placerville, brought over $2,000,000, and White Rock hydraulic mining three miles northeast produced over $5,000,000. Following the ancient tertiary gravel beds, the Franklin Mine east of town produced tons of gravel processed through a 10-stamp mill resulting in large yields from over a 100-foot long sluice run.

The 1857 Cary House

Cary House, built in 1857 by William Cary as an imposing three-story brick hotel, over the years was known as Raffle's Hotel located at 300 Main Street. Centered in downtown Placerville, the hotel has welcomed a golden era of guests to its 77 rooms over its lifetime with legendary guests including Mark Twain, President Ulysses S. Grant, and John Studebaker, and notable folks like William "Buffalo Bill" Cody, Charles Boles or "Black Bart", Levi Strauss, Lola Montez, female Stagecoach driver Charley Parkhurst, movie queen Bette Davis, and Elvis Presley, all visited and stayed there. Horace Greeley, in 1859, famously addressed a crowd of miners

Cary House, in downtown Placerville, was built during the Gold Rush years.

from its veranda and stumping for his campaign run as US President while promoting the transcontinental railroad. After the turn of the century, a fourth floor added, expanded the hotel's size with renovations revealing a hidden cache of gold dust and nuggets discovered during the construction. Today, the hotel features 40 rooms with larger suite sizes.

GOLD BUG MINE

Hangtown's Gold Bug Park is a 61-acre historical park situated within City of Placerville at 2635 Gold Bug Lane, and located 9/10 of a mile north of Highway 50 off Bedford Avenue. Once dotted with over 250 mines, the Park is developed and preserved as an historical site. Visitors may enter a 352 foot long horizontal shaft on tours into the actual Gold Bug Mine to 'get the feel' of the Gold Rush era. It remains open for general admission for tours every day of the week after April, and on weekends during winter. Visitors enjoy picnics, hiking along two miles of trails, and panning for gemstones! Though the mining in the area began in 1849, the Hattie Mine operations started in 1888. In 1926, the Gold Bug Mine continued operating through WW II. Using the original name of the mine, the Hattie Museum & Gift Shop opened in 1996. The Gold Bug Park gift shop and the Joshua Hendy Stamp Mill Museum are staffed by knowledgeable volunteers. 530-642-5207.

US Highway 50 Corridor – El Dorado County

El Dorado County Historical Museum
Adjacent to the El Dorado County Fairgrounds at 104 Placerville Dr., the historical museum offers train rides on tracks built by the Southern Pacific Railroad line making round trips of 40 to 45 minutes, from stations between the 1896 depot at 4241 Mother Lode Drive in Shingle Springs, to 4650 Oriental Street in El Dorado. Rides are available on Gang Cars, once used by inspectors and officials. Hours: Wed-Fri by reservation, call 530-621-5865.

Fountain & Tallman Soda Factory Museum
Run by the El Dorado Historical Society as a unique rock rubble style construction with two-foot thick walls built between 1852-53 at the site of John Fountain & Benjamin Tallman's Soda Works. The museum is located at 524 Main St., Placerville, and open Sat-Sun 12-4PM, call 530-626-0773.

Coloma
Of the earliest El Dorado County settlements, the gold discovery site in Coloma at Sutter's Mill is located on the American River's South Fork and a short ride from Placerville, via State Highway 49. The first breaking news of a California gold strike after James Marshall's sighting of gold nuggets was confirmed,

Sacramento Gold Country

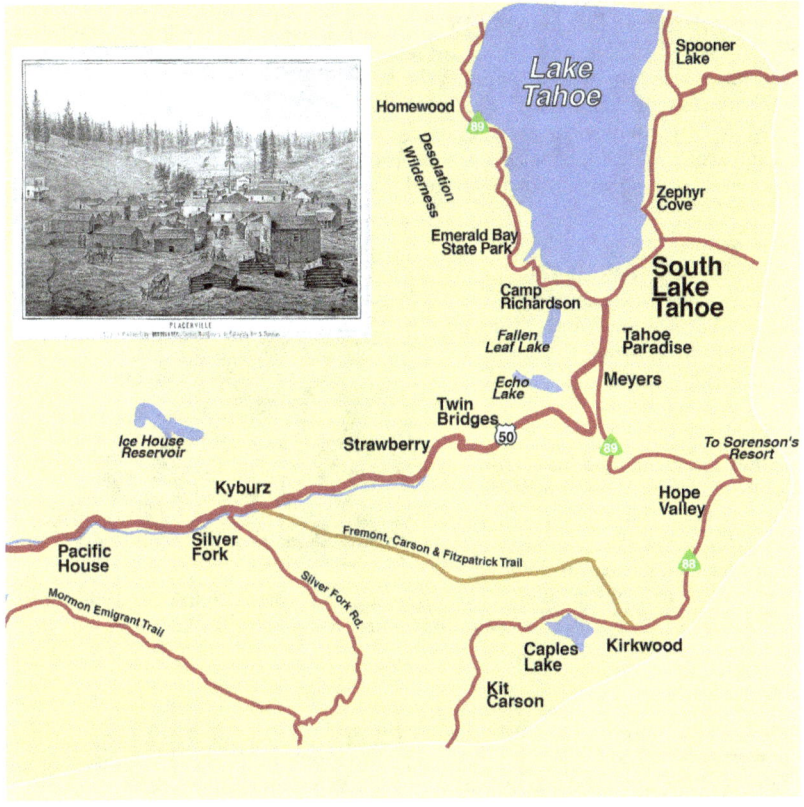

PLACERVILLE

reaching San Francisco early in 1848. El Dorado County became the central hub with hoards of migrants arriving in a mounting momentum to following the creeks and streams in prospecting for gold along the rivers.

Lotus

Uniontown was one and a half miles downstream from Coloma and named by miners soon after James Marshall's nearby gold discovery. The early settler Adam Lohry, a German tailor, built a general store and personal residence there in the 1850s of red brick. He suggested the town's name of Lotus, later adopted by the Post Office in 1881. The old general store is now Adam's Red Brick Restaurant and reportedly haunted.

Georgetown

10 miles northeast of Coloma, 19 miles from Auburn, 26 miles from Folsom Lake State Recreation Area, the mining town of Georgetown became an established gold camp in 1848, tucked away in a steep canyon above the American River. Of legendary placer diggins, Georgetown's early miners sluiced gold finds known as "growlers" due to their giant size, panning out nearly $20,000 in the first six weeks. The first camp consequently was nicknamed

"Growlersburg". In December of 1849, the town mushroomed to over 3,000 encampments and became known as Georgetown Diggins. During work on the Georgia Slide seam deposits, miners shortened the name to Georgetown. In 1852, a disastrous conflagration destroyed the entire town and moved further up Main Street where the town rebuilt its present-day location. The downtown main street was designed with a unique 100-foot width layout from side to side, and street parking within its center median.

Camino

At the US Highway 50, Camino, on the way between downtown Placerville and South Lake Tahoe has several notable wineries and an historic hotel in the area.

Cool

A small village named for Aaron Cool, approximately five miles from the North and Southern Forks of the American River. The town lies at the Highway 49 junction on the main road leading to Georgetown. A placer mining and tent camp in the 1850s, Cool established in 1885 an extensive millon-dollar town boardwalk and promenade, with its Post Office.

The Camino Hotel, US Highway 50.

Kelsey

Neighboring Coloma, the town of Kelsey is the remote hamlet of Kelsey Canyon and named for Benjamin Kelsey, who found rich placers at Kelsey Diggings. The first gold discoverer, James W. Marshall ran a blacksmith shop just south of town and now California Historical Landmark 319. To the rear of the shop are tunnels of the Old Grey Eagle Quartz Mine dug back to 200 feet. Marshall resided at the Union Hotel in Kelsey, a place where he spent his declining years until 1885. In 1864, the Cincinnati and Mansfield companies produced one, then two million after installing a 15-stamp water-powered stamp mill. By 1871, a steam-driven 20-stamp mill had replaced it. Around three-quarters of a mile south, Marshall had located the Big Sandy Mine. A 10-stamp mill was active there in the 1890s, later producing excellent specimens of crystallized gold into the 1930s. Historical spots include the Pioneer Museum, the Blacksmith Shop, Tom Allan's Saloon, and Pioneer Cemetery.

Garden Valley

An early gold camp, Garden Valley is located between Coloma and Georgetown, at the junction of Irish and Empire creeks. It's Post Office was established in 1852. In 1857, a nugget found there was valued at $525. The Rosecrans Mine was worked until 1888 and reactivated in 1916 and 1918, then again in the 1930s. The nearby Black Oak Mine produced well over a million by 1942. It is said, the town came from the settlers finding profits raising and selling vegetables, in the place of a gold mining career.

Diamond Springs

Three miles south of Placerville, Diamond Springs was a rich placer mining spot and yielded a 25 lb. nugget dug out by early miners. The town was known for crystal clear spring waters located along the north side of Main Street. Diamond Springs once rivaled the activities of Placerville from its population of 8,000 in the 1850s, and today there are still a few of the early stone buildings survived from the fires that frequently swept through the area at the time.

Shingle Springs

About 11 miles from Placerville, Shingle Springs named in 1849 for its shingle mill production of 16,000 shingles per day supplying the area's buildings. A well of very cold water refreshed the travelers along the overland Carson Emigrant Trail. The historic Shingle Spring House is the oldest building built in 1850, located at the side of the well.

Pilot Hill

Pilot Hill, a promontory landmark oversees the surrounding ravines and hills. A large fire-beacon at its summit once guided wagons to and from Sacramento Valley. 17 miles from Georgetown, Pilot Hill stands between the Middle and South Forks of the American River in El Dorado County. This area proved rich with placer mining early in 1849 and by 1856, water channeled from the Pilot and Rock Creek Canal reached the mining camps. Within a year, two miners discovered a boulder 'literally gorged with gold'. With one sample assayed in San Francisco valued at $1,760, eventually the boulder sold for $8,000. By 1902, Pilot Hill was considered the center of the local quartz mining district. At first, a 10-stamp mill was installed about 6 miles southwest on the American River's east side and later was increased to a 20-stamp, producing by 1901 record yields of $1,000,000. Later, the mill was consumed by fire and activity slowed by 1941. In 1956, the US Government inundated the surrounding area for Folsom Dam. Surviving historical buildings stand today and the Bayley House from 1862, an impressive 3-story brick edifice of 10,000 sq. ft., was an exquisite hotel with 22 rooms with a winding circular staircase leading to the top grand ballroom. Look for improvements and future renovations for the progress of the Bayley House.

The Placerville Boeger Winery features fine wine tasting in their root cellar display room.

Mud Springs Trading Post and Hotel

Four miles southwest of Placerville along the Carson Emigrant Trail leading to 'The Lake Of The Sky', James Thomas began a trading post and hotel during the fierce winter of 1849, naming it the Mud Springs House. Mud Springs was a cattle and horse watering hole with the wet soil muddying up an entire standing herd. It was a significant stopover from Lake Tahoe for pioneers crossing over from the Sierra Emigrant Trail. The El Dorado Mud Springs Trading Post was an important remount spot for the Overland Pony Express Station in the 1860s in delivering mail to and from St Joseph, Missouri. The Post Office was established in 1854 and recorded 2,500 residents. On the way to Sacramento, the route branches towards a once tumultuous camp of Hangtown, or today's Placerville, south along Highway 49 reaching the first Central Mines of Plymouth, Amador City, and Drytown.

El Dorado National Forest

Located on the western Sierra Nevada slope east of Placerville, a preserve of 596,724 acres offers fishing, boating, river running, swimming, camping, hiking, riding trails, winter skiing, snowmobiling and picnic sites. Fallen Leaf Lake within the Desolation Wilderness is open year-round by permit. 530-303-2412

Kyburz – Trails, Camping, Lodging

A pastoral settlement from 1858, 20 miles from Lake Tahoe along Highway US 50 near the Emigrant Pass. The Kyburz Hotel sprung up as a cabin built in the area called Slippery Ford, and the original cabin was expanded with a large fireplace and named the Sugarloaf Hotel at the time. Strawberry Lodge settled the area with a grand hostelry of lodging with 42 rooms and more conveniences for visitors to the El Dorado Forest Area. A National Watchable Wildlife site for migrating birds lies southeast at the Kyburz Marsh Interpretive Area with a road east linking additional forest roads, fire lookout towers, also a great mountain biking and hiking region.

Pollock Pines – Sly Park Recreation Area

A beautiful area offering camping, picnicking, hiking, equestrian trails. Jenkinson Lake at Sly Park Recreation Area on the American River has fishing and boating. As water was a precious commodity for mining gold in the early 1850s, the South Fork Canal Company was formed in 1852 there using a four-feet wide by three-and-a-half deep wooden flume, using canvas joints set at a four-foot grade over one mile.

Desolation Wilderness Area

A natural preserve nearly 100-square miles and run by the US Forest Service, with wilderness permits required. Adjacent and west of Lake Tahoe within El Dorado National Forest, several lakes, streams, and waterfalls with camping, hiking, and backpacking are accessed following the old Carson Emigrant Trail exploring from Highway 50 Desolation Wilderness and nearly 150 lakes and smaller ponds, including Fallen Leaf Lake and Round Lake with many other well-known destinations, info: 530-644-2340.

75

II. Northern Gold Country
Tour 5
Sacramento, Nevada, El Dorado, Placer Counties

Lake Tahoe view from Heavenly Ski Resort, in South Lake Tahoe.

Exploring the 'Lake of the Sky'
California State Parks Camping and Info: **800-444-7275**
Lake Tahoe US Forest Service Headquarters: **530-543-2600**

The legendary Tahoe Blue appeared to John C. Frémont during his first famous topographical expedition crossing the Rockies and Sierra Mountains in 1844. He encountered an immense mountain lake measuring over 190-square miles, but never located the spillway traveling inland 106-miles towards its landlocked destination in Nevada at Pyramid Lake. Lake Tahoe is a natural Sierra Nevada mountain wonder and largest freshwater lake at the elevation level of 6,225 feet. From its depth reported at over 1,600 feet, Tahoe is the largest natural alpine lake in the country, measuring around 22 miles long by 12 miles wide. Counting the five Great Lakes in the central United States, Lake Tahoe ranks next in line of volume for fresh water sources. In and around Lake Tahoe, corridors of smaller lakes and streams feeding the rivers of the Sierra Nevada watershed into wide canyons and valleys with the potential of several eye-opening expeditions. To reach Lake Tahoe from Golden Chain Highway 49 in Jackson or Angels Camp, each junctions with an approach to the east at Ebbetts, Monitor and Carson Pass connectors into the Sierra Nevada Mountains, from State Highway 88 or State Highway 4. In perfect timing with foothill Fall foliage, these roads reveal a magical beauty in the Sierra high-alpine highway passing Silver Lake,

8 miles from Tahoe City, the winter venue of 1960 in the mountains known as Palisades Tahoe in Olympic Valley featuring extensive mountain lifts, lodging, and shops.

Caples Lake, and Kirkwood Ski Resort. Across the hills of the Carson River Pass and over the Sierra Nevada Mountains where Highway 88 meets Highway 89, the direction to Lake Tahoe follows the old historical Emigrant Trail along US 50. Along the way, make a stop at Hope Valley's famous fly fishing resorts and enjoy a natural year 'round getaway with relaxing rustic cabins. US Highway 50 through El Dorado County follows the American River into the El Dorado National Forest and touches Emerald Bay Road, passes Myers, Kyburz Pass, Strawberry, Echo Lake, Desolation Wilderness at Fallen Leaf Lake. Other points of interest begin from Highway 49 and the Sierra Scenic National Byway, accessing Lake Tahoe from Nevada City and Grass Valley. Take the I-80 at the State Highway 20 exit, at Spaulding Lake Campground and Bowman Lake Road. Nearby, a steep dirt roadway up to Grouse Ridge is a high altitude fire outlook vantage point and access to the Granite Chief Wilderness, with incomparable views of the Sierra Nevada Foothill watershed and valleys below.

Sierra powder found at Sugar Bowl.

Skiers take to the slopes at the Heavenly ski lift downtown in South Lake Tahoe.

TAHOE CITY
Originally, a lumber center and the first permanent settlements on the lake, the Tahoe House was erected in 1863. The Grand Central Hotel followed in accommodating visitors into the area. A walkabout the town uncovers many hidden shops, great food, and lakefront views.

LAKE TAHOE HISTORICAL MUSEUM
The Lake Tahoe Historical Society at 3058 US Highway 50 in historical South Lake houses a museum featuring Tahoe's first inhabitants, the Washoe Indians and covers the settlements once part of the Comstock Silver Rush. Find histories showcases on Snowshoe Thompson, the Pony Express, railroads, steamships, the Lincoln Highway, and gaming industry on display. The Museum's bookstore carries a large collection of titles on Lake Tahoe and western history. Thurs–Sat. 11AM–3PM, between Memorial Day and Labor Day; and Winter hours, Sat–Sun 12–4PM, 530-541-5458.

TALLAC HISTORIC SITE
Emerald Bay Road to Camp Richardson and Heritage Way across from Fallen Leaf Lake Road. Open between Memorial Day weekend through September, the grounds also serve year 'round as a destination for popular cross-country skiing and snowshoeing.

TAHOMA-EMERALD BAY STATE PARK
Located 12 miles north of South Lake Tahoe, hiking to Emerald Bay follows the contour of the north side of the bay for nearly 6 miles out and back. Vikingsholm, Tahoe's hidden castle began in the late 1860s, later expanding in 1929. From the parking lot at Highway 89 on a steep one-mile pedestrian trail that drops 400-feet in elevation, reaches the house acquired by the State of California in 1953. Restrooms and a water fountain are available near the mansion in summer. Tours begin in May. Visitor center, 530-541-6498.

A scenic shoreline view of at the foot of Ski Run Blvd., South Lake Tahoe.

TAHOE RIM TRAIL

Surrounding Lake Tahoe, the Tahoe Rim Trail affords magnificent views of Tahoe Blue and open to all travelers interested in circumnavigating its shoreline, with some restrictions. At an elevation of 4,500 near lake level and higher into the mountains, the 165-mile Rim Trail of Lake Tahoe is considered one of the most premier in the world. Paths perc above the Lake's surface and access the shore from several points of entry both in Nevada and California, each perfect for hiking, biking climbing and spectacular views. The flume trail above the eastern shore is single track view over the lake's crystal waters and follows along the steep lake edge. Dogs are allowed on all sections of the trail with provisions. Red and golden hues of Fall foliage return late September making views from the rim a colorful destination for all sightseers.

THE EAGLE POINT CAMPGROUND

Upper Eagle Point Campground and Emerald Bay Boat Camp are open for seasonal reservations. Eagle Falls and Eagle Lake are two-mile round trip hikes on the Rubicon Trail accessed from Highway 89 at the Eagle Falls Picnic Area or DL Bliss State Park.

D.L. BLISS STATE PARK

Adjacent to Emerald Bay State Park on Lake Tahoe, D.L. Bliss is a California State Park created in 1926. A notable feature, the Rubicon Point Light is the highest elevation lighthouse in the US. There is sightseeing, hiking, swimming, camping, and fishing.

Gabriel suspends above while climbing Cave Rock at Lake Tahoe.

Northern Gold Country

SUGAR PINE POINT STATE PARK
Sugar Pine Point in Tahoma is a forested area on the western shore of Lake Tahoe, with a sandy beach and pier. General Creek Campground is the largest on the lake's western shore and features 175 campsites. A great locaton for wimming, fishing, hiking, sightseeing, cross-country skiing, and biking.

ECHO SUMMIT
SOUTH LAKE TAHOE
Once known as Nebelhorn, Echo Summit offers downhill skiing, chairlifts, ski shop, rentals, and cafeteria. Groomed and tracked cross-country trails, with rolling to mountainous terrain.

SIERRA SKI RANCH
2,000 acres, featuring cross-country and downhill skiing off US 50, with ski lifts, rentals, and cafeteria.

HEAVENLY VALLEY AT SOUTH LAKE TAHOE
Downhill skiing, ski lifts, snowmaking, a ski shop, rentals, restaurants, tram, cafeterias, 530-541-1330.

SNOWFEST
The 10-day Mardi Gras celebration, SnowFest began in 1982 as an annual tradition every March, held throughout the towns of North Lake Tahoe. Activities are available to all ages with parades, fireworks, snow golf tournaments, snow sculpture contests, the crowning of the Queen and King, ski races, parties, concerts, performances, kid-friendly activities, polar bear swim, dog and pet events, music, and fireworks. Local restaurants, bars, and businesses join in the fun. As one of the largest winter mountain events on the West Coast, the mission supports local nonprofits, public programs, student organizations, and scholarships throughout its ten-day celebration. Admission varies with each event and many free, visit www.snowfest.org for more information.

View of Lake Tahoe at Cave Rock.

TOUR 6
PLACER COUNTY
OLD AUBURN CROSSROADS

At the Nevada St. Exit, near the I-80 junction of State Highway 49, and the historic Old Auburn downtown just north of the American River and Sutter's Mill.

In the pioneer tradition, Old Auburn would grow around a crossroads as the hub to five old wagon-pack trails, with converging forty-niner immigrants on the way into the Sierra Nevada Foothills Northern Mines, Lake Tahoe, or rush to the Comstock mines in Nevada of 1859. From Sacramento via I-80 East, make a a 30 mile drive to Auburn's Gold Rush district on a journey to the end of a golden rainbow, discovering a trove of unique shops, lodging, museums, and restaurants overshadowed only by the towering statue at the I-80 entry in honor of the founding father prospector, Claude Chana.

From downtown, Highway 49 leads into the Auburn Ravine State Recreation Area and follows the confluence of two forks of the American River with a 20-mile access to the river, between Auburn and Colfax. Recreational adventures lead to river access, swimming, hiking, boating, fishing, camping, mountain biking, gold

The 1894 Auburn Courthouse.

panning, with limited hunting, equestrian trails, whitewater rafting, and off-road motorcycling. The habitat of seasonal wildflower blooms include monkey flowers, fiddleneck, Indian paintbrush, larkspur, lupine, and brodiaea in settings from chaparral within the ravine wall canyons. Forests of Ponderosa pines, Douglas Fir, Black Oak, Madrone trees fill the foothill woodlands with groves of alders, willows, cottonwoods and creek dogwoods along the stream banks.

Originally Wood's or North Fork Dry Diggins was applied, but prospectors traveling from the nearby Bear River at Sicard's Ranch in May 1848, had migrated from Auburn, New York and gave the camp its place name. Old trails served farming, trading, transportation, railroads, water flumes, and stagecoach routes to reach the earliest Gold Rush settlements. Eventually, all roads were superseded with early turnpikes and toll roads. Early Gold Rush settlement claims

Auburn's historic firehouse is the landmark sentinel since 1891, located in old downtown Auburn.

purchased as individual plots at 20 x 30 feet were based on rumors a man might make $1,000 to $1,500 a day placer mining on the riverfront and living in tent camps like Beal's, Doton's, Smith's, Horseshoe, Rattlesnake, Beaver, Milk Punch, Deadman's, Lacy's, Manhattan, and Tamaroo Bar among the many islets and river bars along the American River. After winter storms washed away sites buried out of sight, the lure to Auburn used on maps for its rich paydirt and as a vital transportation center. Afterwards, the more powerful modern 'hydraulicking' operations methodically reclaimed previous mines in the 1880s, washing and sluicing out gold and supplying water in flumes from high-elevation mountain lakes and steams.

The Travelers Rest Hotel, a dedicated Gold Rush museum on the Auburn-Folsom Road, connects Coloma at Sutter's Mill 17 miles, south on Highway 49. In 1851, a residence, winery, and wine-processing building with a carriage barn was operated by Bishop & Long through 1858. One of the oldest historic buildings in town, the hotel served as the Bishop's home until 1864, then sold

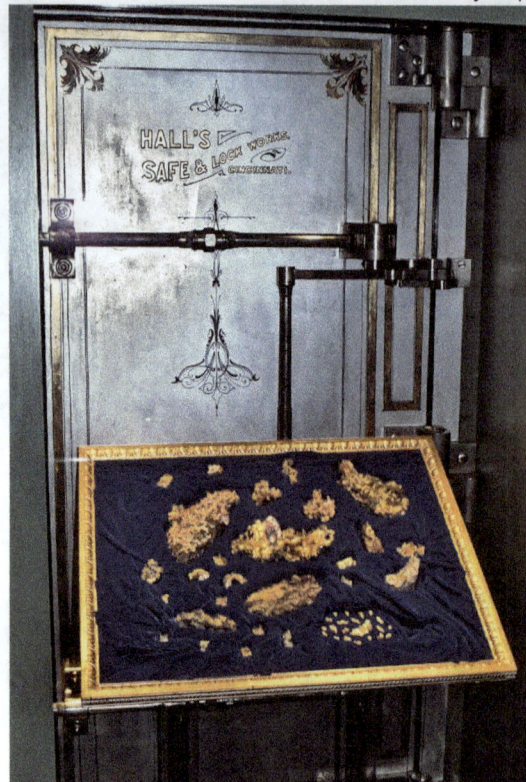

Gold ore displays at the Placer County Museum in the Auburn Courthouse.

at public auction in 1868. Bernhardus Bernhard, a native of Germany, purchased the property for a sum of $3,500. Starting out in St. Louis with a wife and child, he settled his family in Auburn. He gained employment as a teamster driving freight, and the house became a family home with six children and expanded in 1870.

The downtown Post Office from 1849 is one block from the iconic Firehouse of 1891, and each are within walking distance of the 200 Sacramento Street Joss House Museum and Chinese History Center, from 1909. On the hilltop above, the Placer County Courthouse completed in 1894, houses the Placer County Museum and displays many historic cultural and Gold Rush artifacts. The collection of placer gold ore exhibits sizable nuggets of the early days. Also, its collection of artifacts is a stellar repository of native crafts and art of the Southwest, and Northwest Coast, Alaska, with eastern items on the first floor of the historic Placer County Courthouse at 101 Maple Street. Placer County Museum is open Tuesday through Sunday from 11AM to 4PM, with free admission. The Docent Guild provides a historical Guided Walking Tour of Old Town Auburn every Saturday at 10AM. Meet a docent on the Courthouse steps for a one-hour walking tour. Call, 530-889-6500.

The Gold Country Museum

The Gold Country Museum at 1273 High Street is a part of the Auburn Gold Country Fairground and at the rear of the main building. The museum exhibits include a reconstructed mine and offer gold panning in an original WPA-era facility. The grounds display mining equipment, a walk-through tunnel, operational stamp mill, gold panning, tent saloon, and Faro table. For guided tours, call 530-823-4533.

It's easy visualizing yesteryear's excitement and merriment ending the day at 49er miner's gatherings in Old Town Auburn.

PLACER COUNTY HISTORICAL SPOTS

OPHIR
Spanish Corral, three miles west of Auburn was renamed after the source of biblical gold adorning the temple of Solomon. Ophir became the most populated mining camp in Placer County in 1852 and historically is the chief quartz gold mining center of Placer County.

GOLD RUN
Off I-80, initially Mountain Springs, the hydraulicked diggins of Gold Run lies atop a ridge above the Bear River and the American River South Fork. A tent camp established by O. W. Hollenbeck in 1854 is a historical landmark for widespread mining. The operation produced around $6,125,000 in gold between 1865-1878. By 1884, lucrative earnings terminated after the Sawyer ruling against hydraulic mining, causing its suspension and abandonment.

CLIPPER GAP
In June 1865, with the first leg of the transcontinental railroad completed from Sacramento at Clipper Gap, the California Stage Company transportation line stopover continued trips to Lake Tahoe and Virginia City, Nevada. An iron ore mining site discovered by Pennsylvanians found large boulders containing rich amounts of the mineral. In 1857, tests proved the ore to be of high quality, and mining began in earnest in 1869, shipping its production to San Francisco. By 1880, a smelting plant erected remains with some old buildings.

COLFAX

Colfax was named for U. S. Senator Schuyler Colfax who visited there in 1865 during the construction of the transcontinental railroad. Originally a prosperous mining region and trading center in the old town site of Illinoistown, Colfax first settled in 1849 as Alder Gulch. Colfax offers a sprawling and diversified village of shops, antique stores, restaurants, and lodging choices. The Colfax Heritage Museum at 99 Railroad Street and Church Street is a model revival 'Colonnade-style' depot from 1905 with a growing collection of railroad memorabilia on exhibit from the original Central Pacific Railroad transcontinental line. Call, 530-346-8599.

DUTCH FLAT

An old mining town and an important stage stop, Dutch Flat is just halfway between Lake Tahoe and Sacramento, and known once as Dutch Charlie's. In an area of hydraulic mining, thousands of migrants and the Chinese population reached over 2,000 settling there during railroad construction days. The largest California voting population was living in Placer County by 1860, and its prominence grew in peak production periods with the timber industry expansion above the American River, and the newly installed transcontinental railroad. Exhibiting from a "Golden Triangle" encompassing Dutch Flat, Gold Run, Alta, and Towle, the Golden Drift Museum in the center of downtown is open at 32820 Main Street. For info, 530-389-2126.

EMIGRANT GAP

Over 5,000 feet in elevation, the headwaters of the Bear River region brought yields amounting to $1,000,000 in ore during the 1930s. It had an old lumber camp and station on the Central Pacific Railroad at the site where the old Emigrant Trail at Bear Valley leads into Nevada City.

IOWA HILL

An 1853 discovery site for ore had produced by 1856 around $100,000, then by 1880 yielded $20,000,000 in gold. Rebuilt after several fires and again consumed by fire in 1922, it turned into a ghost town.

No Hands Bridge, American River.

FORESTHILL DIVIDE

The active mining area located between the North and Middle Forks of the American River is a peninsula of thickly forested land. It became the most productive cement-tunnel mining district in the State, with a total output reaching $10,000,000 in 1868. The Foresthill Divide Museum at 24601 Harrison Street, at the Leroy Botts Memorial Park presents historical Foresthill and Iowa Hill Divide, displaying many Gold Rush artifacts, a logging exhibit, and scale model of the lumber mill with educational displays on Native Americans, recreation, and transportation, as well as rotating and permanent exhibits on the area encompassing Dutch Flat, Gold Run, Alta, and Towle. The museum at 32820 Main Street, Foresthill, is open Memorial Day through Labor Day Weekends, Sat–Sun, 12PM-4PM. 530-889-6500. Special Tours are available.

FORESTHILL BRIDGE & NO HANDS BRIDGE

The Foresthill Bridge is accessed from I-80 outside of Auburn and over the ravine, it's length of 2,428 feet crosses the river at 730 feet above ground level. The bridge spans the American River North Fork and is the third-highest bridge nationally. Just downstream, No Hands Bridge, a landmark cement arched crossing on the American River North Fork at the Auburn Ravine, was built as a railroad bridge in 1910.

NEWCASTLE

The Victorian-era fruit packing sheds were home to an important railroad depot of the Central Pacific Railroad and well known in local history. At the head of Secret Ravine, the area mined for gold in Secret Diggings was a camp consisting of tents and shanties. Within two years, the District's population soared to 1,500 becoming a large producing placer mining site. Chinatown and the Old Newcastle Market Place are touring destinations there.

PENRYN

The Griffith Quarry Park and Museum on 23 acres surrounds the original two-story building made of granite blocks from the remaining quarry and polishing mill, residing at the corner of Taylor & Rock Springs Rds. The quarry is a California Historical Landmark listed on the National Register of Historic Places as a granite quarry and produces some of the highest-density granite used in construction throughout the State.

ROCKLIN

First recognized as a destination along the transcontinental railroad, the Rocklin area was known for high-density granite mined in town after 1864. It is home to the main campus of Sierra College.

ROSEVILLE

Established in 1864, the town of Junction would grow to Roseville, centered around the railyard junction to the transcontinental railway. Its population grew to a modernized suburb and full-service community of restaurants, lodging, old downtown antique shops, and peripheral shopping malls. The California State Archives is located at 201 N. Sunrise Ave. There is a community center, library, and Veterans Memorial Rose Garden. The 152-acre Maidu Regional Park offers a small museum and indigenous historical sites.

Snowshoe Thompson pioneered mail delivery throughout the Sierra.

TOUR 7
NEVADA COUNTY

NEVADA CITY & GRASS VALLEY GETAWAY

The calendar may read differently, but all around the Northern Sierra Gold Rush towns of Nevada County it looks and feels like California of the 1850s. In Auburn on Highway 49, follow the Golden Chain trail 23 miles to the Northern Mines region of Grass Valley and Nevada City. Festivities and events frequently draw visitors each year to the antique villages as popular destinations for shopping, dining, live music and arts, recreation, and sightseeing tours. Nevada City and Grass Valley are sister towns just five miles apart, and far from busy interstate highways. Make

Vivid autumn colors preceeding cool Sierra weather cycles of snow and rain in Nevada City.

the trip along two-lane roads and enjoy the extensive recreational opportunities amid verdant forests, lakes, and rivers on the Sierra National Scenic Byway. Highway 49 leads to the northern Gold Rush towns of Victorian architecture, stately churches, museums, and village parks to amble in. Travelers find real gold mines, vintage equipment, tools, unique narrow-gauge railroading and mining artifacts along with historical tours. Over the years, artists, and musicians settled in the twin towns and harmoniously exist with presentations at several entertainment centers. Ever-evolving arts and cultural visuals around town are a showcase to visitors and residents alike with art galleries, live music, and theater performances on several stages in town at local night spots. An abundance of choices include shops, restaurants, local breweries, and wineries around each corner of town. Festival goers adore the eminent Constitution Day parade at Nevada City, at the place where the unique tradition began with living history events drawn from characters of the past playing their authentic roles. The second oldest continuous bicycle race in America is synonymous with Nevada City's name, and the world-class race is attended by cheering crowds every summer known for riders climbing the town's hills and facing the tallest, 'The Wall'. Two early Gold Rush establishments, the Holbrooke and the National hotels, are among the most venerable consistently operated hotels in the State, each with an authentic saloon from the Gold Rush days. The towns have few stop-and-go intersections and fewer if any traffic lights! Historic bed and breakfast inns are available within the residential streets of theaters, shops, and high-quality restaurants, all within walking distance in town.

Where the Past is Always Present

In 1848, 'Caldwell's Upper Store' and 'Deer Creek Dry Diggins' became the adopted place names used by the earliest settlers before Nevada became used with its incorporation in 1850 and reflecting on its snow-laden winters. The county seat of Nevada County, Nevada City, was just 'Nevada' during the earliest years and the 'City' was added afterwards, once the Nevada Territory next door became organized as a State.

Nevada City's downtown Firehouse #1 from 1861.

The moniker, "Queen City of the Northern Mines" earned by its elegance and phenomenal wealth, was highly regarded among the towns during the Gilded Age. Framed in autumnal colors during cooler days, many quaint antique Victorian homes are visible throughout the town streets and follow old winding erratic miners' trails spread over seven prominent hills, with Deer Creek running through the town center. There are 93 historic buildings listed on the National Register of Historic Places in downtown Nevada City, and the immense, recently renovated 1880s Stone Brewery stands on the corner at Broad Street and Sacramento Street, across the town on Deer Creek. Nevada City buildings of the Gold Rush days harbor unique shops and restaurants providing a robust historical town center. Corner gaslights illuminated along the fabled streets lead visitors to friendly shops on Broad Street and award-winning restaurants in outdoor creekside settings. Nevada City's downtown Nevada Theatre from 1865 is considered one of the oldest continuous-running theaters in California and invariably well-attended for its local productions, films, and cultural events. An appearance at the Nevada Theatre by Mark Twain with his humorous monologue was greatly lauded during his brief sojourn during October of 1866 on trips throughout the Gold Country, and commented on by critics as "he displayed not the polish of the finished lecturer –nor did he need it; the crude, quaint delivery was infinitely preferable," and another stated, "His method as a lecturer was distinctly unique and novel. His slow, deliberate drawl, the anxious and perturbed expression of his visage, the apparently painful effort with which he framed his sentences … and all this was original; it was Mark Twain."

Nevada City's annual gathering at Victorian Christmas on Broad Street.

BLACK SAND TURNING GOLD

No matter how large or wide the river, gold panning eventually ran dry at the end of 1849 but not before 40,000 miners accumulated over $20,000,000 in placer nuggets and smaller finds. Both upstream and downstream in the 1850s, resolute miners increasingly were inventing new methods of making higher yields of ore from the flowing river's base aggregate. Gold panning evolved with homespun inventions including sluicing techniques using manual rocker machines, and the 'Long Tom', a larger sluice box trapping the extracted heavy-laden black sands with flakes of heavier gold that lie hidden. Within the groups of miners working at the Diggins, more than 100 men toiled over one stretch of a river bar within a canyon, just a little more than 300 feet of one another and often changing the course of the stream in uncovering rich finds at the bedrock. Waters from the cool streams were a relief when standing in the sun with pans or swinging a pickaxe digging up the rocky bottom. At the day's end, a single plank across two barrels under a tree served as an improvised bar to gather around. Music, merriment, and gambling often occurred under the bright moonlight shining on the white sun-bleached canvas tents for shelter from the rain or snow, and frequent inclement winter storms.

Nevada County's Narrow-Gauge Railroad

The original Ott's Assay Office adjacent to the South Yuba Canal Building currently houses Nevada City's downtown visitor information office.

The Post-1850s Mining In Grass Valley

The migration of miners from Cornwall, England, brought new techniques to the Gold Rush for drilling and excavating at much deeper levels in over-mile-deep tunnels. Cornish miners brought their skills, upgraded tools, mastery, and knowledge to the Empire and Northstar Mines and lasted in production extracting gold ore boring out the hard rock through 1956. After

the Pennsylvania, Union, and Ophir Hill mines consolidated into the Empire Mine, gold ore production increased dramatically. The coverings, foundations, and cutaways remain decayed and visible on walks through individual mine grounds spread within the forests of the Empire Mine State Historic Park. In Grass Valley, people walk unknowingly above nearly 350 miles of tunnels. Methods of extracting gold introduced massive dredges carving out an entire riverbed and efficiently conveyed the aggregate to the stamp mills and final separators. Dredging followed the wandering ancient riverbeds and exposed the quartz gold ledge lode deposits in bedrock. The growth of the mining industry tamed the mighty rivers and diverted them overland through mining tunnels, forcing water to flow into new canyons. The industry employment for mining laborers and the use of large stamp mills to process the river

The side-entrance to the Bourne Summer Cottage at Empire Mine in Grass Valley. The Gold Rush mine produced ore into the 1950s amounting to nearly half of all the underground bullion produced during the entire Gold Rush.

aggregate sluiced out every penny. Environmental hazards became a looming conflict between mines affecting valley farmers, and new legal rulings began regulating the practice of hydraulic mining during the 1880s. Underground mining still operates in several nearby foothill locations while strictly observing environmental laws, as many newer methods have eliminated mining impact. The hazards to agricultural and marine-based natural landscapes debased from the exposure include dangerous processes refining gold that had released untold amounts of mercury and toxic arsenic. Between 1851 and 1852, tons of the mined aggregate produced $80,000,000 of bullion reaching its nadir during the Gilded Age. Upon steady decrease past 1865, gold mining had roughly $18,000,000 of hard rock ore mining returns annually.

'Hydraulicking' became the standard industry-wide after 1870, in harvesting gold at a surface level from remote areas of aggregate gravel and ore. Giant water cannon monitors with gravity-fed water ran downhill through flumes and large pipes to send powerful streams of water washing away entire hillsides. After stamping and sluicing out the wash, many landscapes had been denuded appearing moon-like with scarred faces remaining visible today. The use of powerful hydraulic mining equipment allowed companies to successfully rework previous digs. The process continued for 30 years, impacting and contaminating the soils of the Sacramento and Central Valley farmlands. In 1884, besieged with the flow of mining wastes polluting lakes and streams, the landowners' protest created the first environmental laws of the country, codified by the California State Legislature banning hydraulic mining operations forever.

The original Nevada City Miner's Foundry building on Spring St. is an contemporary cultural center.

Rusted from disuse, the mining machinery at the Northstar Mining Museum.

The office building at Empire Mine and largest producing gold mine in the entire Gold Country.

Nevada County's Old West hospitality welcomes visitors into the great Northern Mines Golden Center. The region reflects richly on an inherited past in both Nevada City and Grass Valley especially during seasonal events enjoyed by visitors and resident onlookers. A Nevada City performing arts center on Spring Street Miner's Foundry Cultural Center, a converted old foundry building, continues offering popular events in the area from its inception as a Victorian Museum, with the launch of locally-supported independent radio station KVMR-FM originating in the 1970s. The community center sponsors student DJs and supports training volunteers beaming a signal in the foothills throughout the Sacramento Valley and into Lake Tahoe. Center for the Arts in Grass Valley became a non-profit alliance offering presentations with nationally known and local artists held at several of the town's public facilities, including the stately 25- acre Nevada County Fairgrounds with arenas, fairground buildings under tall ponderosa pines, with plenty of parking and RV camping facilities. The Nevada County Narrow Gauge Railroad and Transportation Museum on Kidder Street features railcar tours, call 530-470-0920.

A relic of the past, the Rowe Headframe stands in decay after decades of service.

Time Capsules

Grass Valley's first settlers arrived in 1848 after traversing the Emigrant Trail over Donner Pass, to linger along a 'grassy valley' on Wolf Creek. By 1867, the gold-laden mines of Grass Valley grew into the fifth-largest town in California with a population of 13,000. At present, Grass Valley is home to about 13,000 residents. More than a century-and-a-half later, gold mining made Grass Valley the most important gold mining center in California. The Empire Mine alone produced some $960,000,000 in gold during its 107 years of operation. Empire Mine today is a 900-acre State Park. Grass Valley, itself a slice of Americana is where

Northern Gold Country

A rendering by Carol Mathis, daughter of famed Nevada City Gold Country artist George Mathis.

WHEN THE RICH GOT RICHER

According to H.H. Bancroft's history, Grass Valley had the first recognized ore from a discovery made in June 1850. The introduction of the first stamp mill began a productive era of mining. The miner, George McKnight camping in Grass Valley discovered the richest Gold Hill ledge. A few months later, the town population increased from 20 cabins in 1850 to 150 buildings by March 1851. More discoveries of quartz and gold ledges include Ophir Hill, discovered by George D. Roberts in his claim 30 x 40 feet one-mile southeast of the town, and expanded, changing hands to become the largest gold quartz lode-producing mine in California at the present-day site of the Empire Mine Museum. An evolution of stamp mills in Grass Valley was regarded as the proving ground for engineering higher amounts of gold production, but slowed due to poor management, causing the Ophir Hill mine to fail in 1852. That same year Orphir mine ownership was transferred to John P. Rush by auction, with one-half purchased by the Empire Company consisting of ten investors. The Empire Mining Company was incorporated in 1854, yielding over $900,000 in returns. By 1864, yields increased to $1,056,234. Sold again in 1864, two new owners, A.H. Houston and Captain S.W. Lee, bought out the stock of the Empire Company. Within a year, the mine's depth reached perpendicularly 201 feet, averaging $58.80 per ton. In 1865, a thirty-stamp mill was installed, with each stamp weighing 800 pounds at a rate dropping 58 to 65 times a minute, yielding a 40-ton daily capacity. New drainage in the mines was introduced with other improvements in 1867, raising mining costs to $8.60 per ton. The influence of hard rock Cornish Miners had been evident as

'Hydraulicking' was a prominent method exposing the gold ore.

GOLD RUSH HISTORIC PARKS
EMPIRE MINE STATE HISTORIC PARK
10791 E EMPIRE ST, GRASS VALLEY, CA

Approximately 65-miles northeast of Sacramento driving north on Highway 49, the Northern Mining region of sprawling early mining towns begin at Grass Valley, the home to the Empire Mine Historic State Park. Its many buildings, overhead rigs, mining tunnels and equipment yard displays were consolidated from a series of Gold Rush mines removing a remarkable 350,000 lbs. of ore in a century, and the largest and longest running gold mine in the Gold Country. Over 367-miles remain of underground tunnels bored beneath Grass Valley, angling nearly two-miles deep into the bedrock. The Empire production was closed in 1957, and then, reopened in 1975 operating as a California State Historic Park with nearly 900-acres of grounds nestled beneath tall pines and colorful oak trees. On display within the large outdoor equipment yard are a miner's workshop and elevator shaft buildings, with the massive Rowe Headframe on the grounds. The stately Bourne Mansion cottage in the park was built entirely from native stone in 1897, and served as the summer home and gardens of its owner. The park operates all year featuring 'living history' programs on weekends, from May through October, when docents perform period demonstrations of mining operations. The Miner's Picnic remains a local tradition for over 125 years. Locals and visitors greatly appreciate the park's vast recreational grounds for hosting weddings, or casual visits, hiking, dog walking, and mountain biking around the property's historic mining ruins. The State Historic Gold Rush Park operates a small museum and bookstore.

Hours: Summer, 10AM–5PM, Winter, 10AM–4PM. Outdoor Trails, 7AM–8PM.
530-273-8522

The Equipment Yard at the Empire Mine.

early as 1861, who were relied on almost exclusively. After the devastation from the fire of 1870, the mine changed hands to Mr. Nesmith as superintendent, who reopened a new gold-bearing ledge, producing a value of $35 to $40 a ton. A new 20-stamp mill operating with 900-pound stamps dropped 9 inches at 72 times per minute, out-performing the 30-stamp mill. By 1874, Empire Mine's shaft depth increased to 1,250 feet with 12 levels and up to 7,900 feet of mine drifts. Ophir Hill closed and flooded after 1878, the company proceeded to mine the Rich Hill vein marking a new turning point. Later, expecting to close, the mine was under the control of the Bourne estate. Its heir, W.B. Bourne Jr. believed he could turn it into a profitable venture with 'systematic explorations' of the mine. By 1883, the Empire Mine again entered a period of prosperity replacing steam-powered

A vintage Stamp Mill built in sections of 5-stamps, Northstar Mining Museum.

machinery with water power. Twenty new stamps added to a 20-stamp mill began driving at once 40 mills. By 1890, the Empire reworked two original ledges, the Rich Hill and Ophir Hill, and added to several other previous mines, the Rush and Laton ore veins. On return from South Africa, George W. Starr accepted the position as manager of the Empire Mine in 1898. After operating at a loss beginning in 1893, the assessment by Starr instituted several new improvements paying dividends to the company's stockholders. Starr succeeded in implementing systematic plans and remained in charge until 1928. The Empire Mine continued further expanding, purchasing the nearby Pennsylvania Mine with another 20-stamp mill running continuously. By 1914, the mine installed a Westinghouse motor that allowed the hoist to operate down a depth of 7,500 feet. In 1918, a more modern 60-stamp installed was capable of handling five tons of material increasing daily profits. Each stamp weighing 1,575 pounds dropped 7 inches at 102 times per minute.

The Northstar Mining Museum, on Wolf Creek, in Grass Valley.

Machine shop and equipment yard at Empire Mine State Historic Park.

Through the 1920s, Empire Mine's expansion of holdings grew with the purchase of several adjacent mines. In 1929, again changing hands, the new Empire Mine Company added the Northstar Mine to its holdings. An 80-stamp mill began crushing ore transported by a 6,000-foot aerial tram with electric rail cars used in the processing. Despite a national depression during the 1930s, Grass Valley was considered 'the greatest mining town in the West.' After purchasing the Sultana Mine with 18 individual claims, 44 mules worked within the deep levels of the mines and were kept permanently underground. They hauled the ore carts to the stamp mills bringing yields equaling 76,595 ounces, in 1933. In 1955, the Empire was ranked as the third largest producer nationally reaching 11,007 feet in the main shaft. Then, all Empire Mine holdings were sold at auction in 1959. With its purchase by the California State Park system in 1975, Empire Mine State Historic Park in Grass Valley features the Bourne Summer Mansion, placid garden grounds, a museum, equipment yard, bookshop, biking, and hiking trails, with tours and days of living history events on weekends.

The workshop at Empire Mine Yard.

BRIDGEPORT COVERED BRIDGE

Bridgeport Bridge, at the Yuba River South Fork State Park.

At the South Fork Yuba River State Park in Bridgeport, the historic 253-foot-long wooden bridge built in 1862 by David Wood, a sawmill owner, was used by miners crossing the Yuba River's South Fork driving their wagons to the Northern Mines and Comstock Lode in Nevada. Today's Bridgeport Covered Bridge was fully restored, and then replaced next to it by a more modern bridge allowing traffic across the river. The venerable bridge remains the longest, oldest surviving single-span covered bridge in America and built entirely of wood. The bridge was a toll crossing along the Virginia Turnpike and wagon trail between Marysville and Virginia City. There are trails with walkways at the State Park Headquarters and gold panning allowed on the river. Bridgeport is 14 miles from Grass Valley, via Highway 20 West, on Pleasant Valley Road.

HOLBROOKE HOTEL

An imposing Gold Rush brick structure standing on Main Street in Grass Valley from 1852, the Holbrooke Hotel has hosted dignitaries and guests during an enduring lifetime. The Golden Gate Saloon, at the entry of the hotel, is a period bar shipped in 1849 'round the horn' to its present location. The building's elaborate interior brick archways and windows are unique treasures of architecture from the era. As one meanders in the library's great room, basement rathskeller, up the classic staircase, or down the steel-caged elevator from the Presidential and Bridal Suites, each room is decked out with period furnishings and second-floor balconies. Many rooms are titled for the famous hotel guests and include several visiting US Presidents. Be sure to try the patio garden restaurant on the lobby floor.

GOLD RUSH CONTEMPORARY
LOLA MONTEZ AND LOTTA CRABTREE

Lola was known for her exacting demands influencing royal decisions.

In 1853, Lola Montez, originally from Ireland, married King Ludwig of Bavaria, then later fled for her life from Europe moving to Grass Valley during the Gold Rush to start a career as an actress and dancer. She was known to be an extravagant dominating personality, and kept a pet bear inside her house or chained to a tree in the yard. A serendipitous meeting with John and Mary Ann Crabtree occurred after their move to Grass Valley's booming mining town center opening a boarding house on Mill Street close to the Lola Montez house. Their daughter, Lotta Crabtree, a budding performer and singer, often met with Lola and later toured throughout the Gold Country on a meteoric rise as a famous performer. Both performed together to the sound of clinking gold coins tossed against the stage floor, and their success became apparent throughout the region and known for a wonderful evening's entertainment. Lola continued mentoring the young actress and Lotta Crabtree began her storied career, first joining the San Francisco Saloon and Theatre Company in 1856. Later, Lotta moved to the East Coast as a successful performer in Uncle Tom's Cabin and earned great status and recognition. Her career sparked national crazes of the late 1860s, and the 'Lotta Polka' and 'Lotta Gallup' made her an early celebrity. At age 47, in 1889 she suffered a fall during a performance and chose to retire as the wealthiest actress in America. Appearing in one final performance during Lotta Crabtree Day at the 1915 San Francisco Panama-Pacific Exposition, she moved to Lake Hopatcong in New Jersey, then later to her hotel in Boston, The Brewster, until 1924. A successful child of the Gold Rush, she left behind an artist foundation from her philanthropy backed by four million, a fund still extant. Departing San Francisco, she contributed a public fountain and monument on Market Street in 1875, known as Lotta's Fountain. At her insistence, it would be water for both animals and humans, featuring four brass outlets 24 feet high, but after the remodeling of Market Street in 1916 rebuilt at 32 feet high, the fountain was restored again to its original height.

Lotta Crabtree (Library of Congress)

TOUR 8
NEVADA, SIERRA, AND PLUMAS COUNTIES
THE YUBA DONNER NATIONAL SCENIC BYWAY

Old US Highway 40 at the Rainbow Bridge in view of Donner Lake, and connection to the Sierra Nevada Yuba-Donner Scenic Byway, from the I-80 Norden exit.

AUTUMN'S GOLD AND SILVER BONANZAS

Follow the 160-mile loop over the Yuba Donner National Scenic Byway on a colorful trip crossing the South Fork, Middle Fork, and North Fork, of the Yuba River in incredible landscapes. Beginning in Nevada City from State Highway 20 at Highway 49, discover legendary foothill Gold Rush trails to mining towns, museums, recreational landmarks, and wind through the six historic Sierra Bonanza towns known for archaeological, cultural, historical, natural, recreational, and scenic qualities. Highway 49's Golden Chain proceeds aside the riverbanks of the Yuba River, leading upstream to Sierra City and majestic vistas of the 7,818-foot high granite peaks of the Sierra Buttes, only one-and-a-half miles away. Within reach of over 50 forested lakes in the Gold Lakes Basin, travelers experience the restored Kentucky Mine Museum and discover Downieville's historical quaint covered walkways. Fall foliage visible throughout September and October in the Sierra Nevada foothills illuminate the alpine elevations, as far as the eye can see. Spectacular views await the displays of foothill maple forests, higher-elevation aspens' golden appearance, and the Black Oak trees transforming into Halloween's hues of red and amber. Taking Highway 89 into Sierraville, the loop passes the historic Donner Pass retracing

The New York Hotel is reported to have boarded Mark Twain during his circuit when performing across the street at the Nevada Theater in Nevada City.

the tragic footprints and camps of 1847 Donner survivors. Continuing sideways, trails to the east from the scenic byway lead where migrant prospectors arrived in Truckee, and eventually Virginia City, Nevada. The history of the hardship and toil is visible along the I-80 grade from Truckee, where the transcontinental railroad forever changed California's frontier landscape. Returning to Nevada City on I-80, to the State Highway 20 West exit, take the two-lane highway and complete the loop back at the Highway 49 junction.

NEVADA CITY'S TWIN TREASURES OF GOLD AND SILVER FORTUNES

The connection to Nevada City's fame and fortune began with the 1849 Gold Rush. In Nevada City downtown, pause at the National Hotel built in 1852, standing today as the oldest continually operating hotel in California, preserved after dual-lane improvements in the 1960s to Highway 49 were added, taking a section from the old building away. The downtown area's large, ornately styled homes extend an authentic Victorian charm and museum-like atmosphere for visitors. Nevada City's Chamber of Commerce at Coyote and Commercial Streets was originally the assay office of James Ott, who confirmed the June 1859 value of $3000-$5000 per ton for Comstock silver ore. This discovery incited an exodus from the gold mines from 1849 towards the Comstock Lode, south of present-day Reno. Judge Walsh, a Grass Valley mining expert, was first to know and first to go. George Hearst, a successful miner, and father of William Randolph Hearst, is part of the fame and fortune tied to the Yuba Donner Byway. Following Judge Walsh's tip, he sold the rock-solid Le Compton gold mine to buy the multi-million dollar Comstock mine. By winter, he would haul enough of the world's richest ore by mule train to San Francisco to bank $80,000 in freshly minted coins.

The Miners Foundry, on Spring Street, became the largest Gold Country manufacturer of hydropower waterwheels engineered originally by Lester Pelton. Miners Foundry Cultural Center presents contemporary culture, music performances, and festive events. On East Broad Street in Nevada City, was the childhood residence of famed European Opera Star Emma Nevada in 1856, and now a quaint bed and breakfast. Nevada Theater held her farewell concert at the turn of the century. Mark Twain, Lotta Crabtree, and Lola Montez had been each billed at the theater, today serving as a multipurpose venue for movies, live theater, and music events.

YUBA RIVER INDEPENDENCE TRAIL

The tour continues by driving north from Nevada City on State Highway 49, and observing visible scars on both sides of the road are the remains of the 1853 startup hydraulic mine, later outlawed. The California South Yuba State Park begins its steep descent into the South Yuba River Canyon, stretching two miles and arriving at Independence Trail. This full-access trail, created in 1977 under John Olmsted, a Nevada City preservationist with Sequoya Challenge, begins near the park's vintage South Yuba River Bridge, paralleling its more modern concrete predecessor. Start along the path off the roadway at the trailhead just north of the Yuba River Bridge. An information kiosk marks the Independence Trail's trailhead along a level four-mile plus round trip, an easy walk for everyone. During the Gold Rush days, the mining flume carried water from the South Fork of Yuba River for hydraulicking over 6 miles of elevated trails, offering visibility for all hikers, specifically in aiding handicapped hikers in discovering their natural surroundings. America's first wheelchair wilderness trail was conceived and implemented by the local conservationist Olmsted, converting it from the abandoned 1859 Excelsior Mining Canal flume, completed after fifteen years in 1992. The flume once carried water 27 miles to hydraulic gold mines at Smartsville and is now part of the South Yuba River State Park. Just one mile west on the trail from Highway 49 parking, one encounters a three-foot by five-foot old wooden canal trail crossing a waterfall. One-and-a-half miles east of the highway, the oldest surviving wooden bridge

Spanning Nevada and Sierra Counties, the Yuba-Donner National Scenic Byway encompasses stunning recreational areas within the original 1849 Gold Country.

in the Sierra Nevada was made from ten by twelve-inch cedar timbers in 1858, spanning Augustini Creek. Abandoned projects from the Gold Rush days lie further northwest, including the Noyes Tunnel, Jones Bar Bridge, and Miner's Tunnel at the eastern end. Approximately 20 miles from the restored townsite of North Bloomfield and a side trip east from Tyler Foote Road, the tour continues amid barren, man-made, and multi-layered cliffside landscapes blasted with powerful streams of hydraulic water at Malakoff Diggins State Historic Park. The mining town went bust in 1884 after the hydraulic practice became banned, leaving washed moonlit ghost towns with denuded hills and forests, incapable of revegetation for over 150 years. On Highway 49 at French Corral Road, Peterson's Corner Store and Restaurant stands a survivor of the area's legendary gold booms and busts. Due west from Peterson's crossroads, a side trip follows the old Henness Pass Wagon Route to Bridgeport Covered Bridge, a landmark considered the longest single-span wooden covered bridge in the nation. In 1862, the Henness Pass Route led miners onto the Virginia City Turnpike, carrying one-third of the immense freight business to the mushrooming Comstock mines. During the boom years of 1863-64, Bridgeport collected tolls on five million tons hauled between Virginia City, Nevada, Marysville, and the seaport in the Delta below. The restored Bridgeport Covered Bridge connects the ghost town of French Corral to Highway 49 at the western end of the 20-mile-long South Yuba River State Park and a 39-mile stretch of the Wild and Scenic Yuba River.

SIERRA GOLD TURNS SILVER

A few miles past the North San Juan, crossing on the Yuba River Middle Fork, Oregon Creek Covered Bridge was 'busted' twice in 20 years, when the 1861-62 flood removed all Sierra bridges, then by the tragic 1883 dam break. The resulting flood and backwash turned Oregon Creek Covered Bridge sideways. Reattaching the bridge's east end to its west abutment with cables, pulleys,

At the precipice with the Yuba South Fork raging below, Independence Trail follows an old wooden flume perfect for disabled hikers seeking a challenge in the Sierra.

and oxen made it the only known covered bridge turned in reversed directions. Continuing northward on State Highway 49, the Yuba Donner Byway will begin a parallel course along the North Fork Yuba River to Downieville, where it quickly rises from 4,000 to 8,000 feet, in sight of the magnificent Sierra Buttes as a backdrop in Sierra City. A picturesque side trip from Sierra City, Bassetts Station at Gold Lake Road, leads to the high-elevation Gold Lakes Basin, featuring fifty lakes, each with eye-catching golden aspen, willow, and mountain maple. Leaving the Yuba River's North Fork at Yuba Pass, Highway 49 meets State Highway 89 near Sierraville. Continue south, at 5,000 feet in elevation and view the largest open alpine valley in the country, the vast Sierra Valley. Approaching I-80, Highway 89 crosses by the North Fork Truckee River to the site of the Donner Party Camps of 1846-47. It is just seven miles north of Truckee and Donner Lake. Subjected to tragic blizzards of snow had struck pioneers, preventing them from crossing the Sierra summit. Signs, trails, and a Pioneer Museum at Donner Lake State Park display the intricate architecture of the Donner Tragedy for visitors. A bronze pioneer statue stands upon a twenty-foot pedestal to equal the snow depths of that terrible winter. Truckee's revived old west railroad town, a century-old travel hub with food and lodging, is on the way to Reno and Lake Tahoe, or the restored Old West town of Virginia City. 'Modern' progress would come in the form of Central Pacific Railroad's first transcontinental trains and their arrival in the summer of 1869, with a main route to Nevada and California, completed just 20 years after the Donner Tragedy. The Big Four railroad barons created the railroad town of Truckee at the junction of routes to Lake Tahoe and Virginia City, Nevada. By the time the world's richest ore of Virginia City was exhausted in 1878, Truckee's journalist and lawyer Charles McGlashan had published the grim details of the Donner Story and created a rich tourist history establishing his first winter ice gardens predating today's ski boom.

Sierra County Henness Pass pioneer trail to the California Gold Rush and Nevada Comstock Lode.

Returning via Old Donner Summit Pass

The Yuba Donner Scenic Byway travels west along the scenic north shore of Donner Lake. Dramatic walls of the Sierra Crest loom over Old US 40, paralleling the early 1844 Stephens Party wagon route and access to Old Donner Pass. The short ascent passes Rainbow Bridge, a landmark near the Pacific Railroad's Chinese Wall and Sierra Crest snow tunnel. At 6,500 feet elevation, the summit crossing of the 2000-mile Pacific Crest Trail from Mexico to Canada creates perfect day hikes, north or south. Old US Highway 40 to Soda Springs from the I-80 junction joins the path of the South Yuba River as it meanders among golden cottonwoods and creek dogwoods at Big Bend Ranger Station. A pioneer logging museum is just before I-80 at Cisco Grove. Four miles further west at I-80's Nevada City exit, State Highway 20 completes the last part of the tour, Bear Valley's glacial meadow, an 1840s rest area for roped-down wagon trains from Emigrant Gap, and the staging area for Donner Party rescue in February-March, 1847. Near the Lake Spaulding Campground off Highway 20, stop at a fascinating study along a short walk on the Sierra Discovery Trail, sponsored by P.G. & E. as an interpretive woodland path, looping through a magnificent old-growth forest, 1/2 mile north on Bowman Lake Road. From the Omega Rest Area, the route descends through giant hydraulic mining scars of the 1860-the 70s, California's 'Second Gold Rush'. By 1884, the Sawyer Decision against North Bloomfield wastes shut most hydraulic mines, curbing the thirty-year devastation of lowland railroad bridges and agricultural destruction while wasting much of the pristine landscape in the Mother Lode.

Nevada City's Yuba Donner Connection

Old US Highway 40 to Soda Springs from the I-80 junction joins the path of the South Yuba River as it meanders among golden cottonwoods and creek dogwoods at Big Bend Ranger Station. A pioneer logging museum is just before I-80 at Cisco Grove. Four miles further west at I-80's Nevada City exit, State Highway 20 completes the last part of the tour, Bear Valley's glacial meadow, an 1840s rest area for roped-down wagon trains from Emigrant Gap, and the staging area for Donner Party rescue in February-March, 1847. Near the Lake Spaulding Campground off Highway 20, find the fascinating study and short walk on Sierra Discovery Trail, P.G. & E.'s interpretive woodland path, which loops through magnificent old-growth forest, 1/2 mile north on Bowman Lake Road. From the Omega Rest Area, the route descends through giant hydraulic mining scars of the 1860-70s, California's 'Second Gold Rush'. By 1884, the Sawyer Decision against North Bloomfield wastes shut most hydraulic mines, curbing the thirty-year devastation of lowland railroad bridges and agricultural destruction while wasting much of the pristine landscape in the Mother Lode.

Nevada County Historical Spots

South Yuba River State Park

The state's first river corridor park headquartered at Bridgeport, is a wide level site of the South Fork of the Yuba River at the Bridgeport Bridge, the longest wooden single-span covered bridge in the nation. Visitors may take part in tours or wander on bird walks, wildflower walks, and enjoy living history on wagon rides and discover gold panning demonstrations and Native American crafts, 530-432-2546.

Travelers encounter a few anomalies along the way on the Golden Chain Highway.

Historic Lola Montez House

The Lola Montez House on Mill St. before its restoration as a tourist information center.

A reproduction faithful to the original home still retains Lola Montez's original door, with the saying, "Whatever Lola wants Lola Gets" grew large after the incident at the Holbrooke Hotel when she reportedly struck a Grass Valley journalist with her whip handle at the Golden Gate Saloon. Lola Montez lived in Grass Valley from 1852-54 and once was courted by European and Russian royalty. She was a mentor to her neighbor, Lotta Crabtree, as their rising stars included many appearances during the Gold Rush at theaters throughout the Sierra Nevada Foothills. Lola was known by the pet bear she kept either inside the house or chained to the tree in the yard.

The North Star Mining Museum

In Grass Valley, the North Star Mining Museum provides a complete look at the hard rock underground mining history in the area. Its outdoor yard display and museum at Wolf Creek is a setting with an old stone factory building at the significant water resource historically used at the Empire Mine. On display, a full-scale model of the underground layout reveals underneath Grass Valley of hardrock mining levels going down to depths over 10,000 feet.

Rough & Ready

The village of Rough & Ready lies seven miles west of Grass Valley on Highway 20 and stands today as a formidable State Historic Landmark of the old Gold Rush days. The city seceded itself from the United States once, and on April 7, 1850, local folks rebelled against government-imposed mining taxes. They

GOLD RUSH HISTORIC PARKS
MALAKOFF DIGGINS STATE HISTORIC PARK
23579 N. BLOOMFIELD RD., NEVADA CITY

From Nevada City, 12-miles north on Highway 49 take the right turn on Tyler Foote Rd., then continue 19-miles past Columbia Hill to arrive at the historic museum town of Bloomfield, at Malakoff Diggins State Historic Park. Nearly 175-years ago surrounded by the Sierra Nevada's rugged mountains, water was harnessed and gravity-fed through huge iron monitors making powerful "Hydraulicking" streams for sluicing gold out of an entire hillside. The landscape at Malakoff State Historic Park is an example of reshaping the surroundings, and was first called Humbug dating back 1852. In 1866, the town of North Bloomfield was established in the canyon adjacent near the ancient river bed at the surface. Named for the Malakoff Tower from the 1874 Crimean War, the mine was fed by an 8,000-foot tunnel carved out from the adjacent South Fork of the Yuba River, making it the world's largest hydraulic site for gold ore recovery. The mining operation used seven giant monitors running 24-hours a day seven days a week, processing 50,000 tons of gravel per day. The practice of washing away hillsides and surface plants, trees, and soil in search of gold has left the hills denuded and virtually unchanged from the Gold Rush era. The miners followed the ancient riverbeds washing out the aggregate into oversized sluices, then readied for the stamp mills. Large gold bars produced at the site were delivered to the mint in San Francisco. The largest bar was said to have weighed 512 pounds and valued at $114,000. The area's population during the Gold Rush years of North Bloomfield, with neighboring camps of Relief Hill, Moore's Flat, Woolsey,

and Orleans Flat, shot up to 2,000 inhabitants. All hydraulic mining operations throughout California were closed in 1884 after the Sawyer decision prohibited the practice. The vintage town and State Historic Gold Rush Park remains open to the public through the year.

Malakoff Diggins (USGS), 530-265-2740.

voted to form their own constitutional republic. However, 'The Great Republic of Rough & Ready' lasted only until the Fourth of July, when Old Glory went up the flagpole and the whole episode passed into history, but not forgotten. Each year, on the last Sunday in June, Rough & Ready hosts a unique and fun-filled Secession Day Celebration. See the Historic District, shops, restaurants and roadside displays. After the fires of 1856 and 1859 all but wiped out the place, there are twenty-four houses left in the town. The Fippin Blacksmith Shop on Highway 20 stands on the road, just outside Grass Valley.

Penn Valley

Downtown Penn Valley began as a stage and freight wagon stop along Highway 20. The area remains today a rural hamlet near the Lake Wildwood championship golf course and small village residential area. Many cattle

The old W.H.Fippin Blacksmith, seen along Highway 20, in Rough & Ready.

ranches and vineyards dot the landscape surrounding the central Western Gateway Regional Park. Every April, the fire department hosts a popular must-see Penn Valley Rodeo.

North San Juan

One block of historic picturesque old buildings with scattered homes are the remnants of a city boasting a population of thousands during the Gold Rush.

French Corral

A ghosty town of historic buildings included the seat of the Milton Mining and Water Company and old Wells Fargo Express office

An old timber hauler on Highway 20, Rough & Ready.

equipped with iron doors still standing. The first long-distance hook up for telephone was invented here.

North Columbia

Historic buildings and aerial landscapes of farming where the old schoolhouse from 1875 is turned into a Cultural Center with an outdoor amphitheater and regular events, at 17894 Tyler Foote Rd. Originally, in Columbia Hill, older

The longest single-span nationally, the old Bridgeport Covered Bridge straddles the South Yuba River leading towards Highway 49, French Corral, and Henness Pass.

homes still stand near the scarred landscapes of hydraulic mining in the sparse looking desert area of Badger Hill Diggings. For information, 530-265-2826.

Malakoff Diggins
State Historic Park
A Gold Rush Park and the largest of all hydraulic mines opened at Malakoff Diggins with hydraulic mining operations or 'Hydraulicking' on display from the mid-1880s. The main town there is North Bloomfield surrounded by entire hillsides washed away from mining gold with high-pressurized water from the mountains. Campfire programs, historic walks and gold panning.

North Bloomfield
Once a mining camp called Humbug, the buildings have been renovated as a museum located at the Malakoff Diggins State Historic Park in North Bloomfield. Visit the huge canyons made from hydraulic mining over 100 years ago. Tours and exhibits of an authentic mining town, 530-265-2740.

Graniteville
A severe fire swept through in 1878, but because hydraulic-mining companies had reservoirs in the mountains above the town, Graniteville was rebuilt. Access to Jackson Meadows, and Bowman Lake area via Tyler Foote Road.

Washington
Yuba River access, rafting, kayaking. Situated on the bank of the South Fork of the Yuba River. Just outside the town are immense piles of huge granite boulders carried there stone by stone, by Chinese miners of Gold Rush days.

Northern Gold Country

Donner Memorial & Summit
Campsites, swimming, fishing and boating. The Donner Party tragedy occurred during the winter of 1846-1847. Of the eighty-one persons who began the winter at Donner Lake and on Alder Creek, thirty six perished in one of the worst snow storms in thirty years. A tablet was placed on Emigrant Trail by the Historic Landmarks Committee which describes the route then followed. Sno-Park Cross-country ski area. No snow play is available. Access is from the Castle Peak Exit off Interstate 80, beyond the Boreal on the south side of the freeway.

Norden
Cross Country Ski trails at Royal Gorge are operated at Rainbow Lodge, off the Big Bend Exit of I-80. Nearby, the Sugar Bowl Ski Area and Rainbow Bridge overview, with its spectacular view of Donner Lake, are off I-80 at the Norden Exit leading along old Highway 40.

Soda Springs
Cross Country skiing and recreational area, off Interstate 80.

Grouse Ridge
Access from Bowman Lake Road on Highway 20 east of Nevada City near Interstate 80, exits 20 miles from Truckee. There are campsites, a boat launch, beach and swimming here and at nearby Lake Fuller. Grouse Ridge Road fire outlook is reached from a steep road to a spectacular a high Sierra panoramic view over the western slope of the Sierra towards Sacramento.

Nevada City Landmarks

The Gault Bridge

The Pine Street Gault Bridge spans Deer Creek, in Nevada City.
(Library of Congress)

In Nevada City, Gault Bridge is an engineering marvel spanning over Deer Creek, on Nevada City's old highway to Grass Valley. It's a local legend and the oldest three-hinge steel-arch bridge in California. A rare surviving example of this type of bridge construction originally designed by the American Bridge Company, the Gault Bridge was erected in 1903 by Clark and Henery, a Stockton, California construction firm and entered into the National Register of Historic Places for its significant role in bridge technology in California.

Grass Valley / Nevada City
Northern Mining Towns and Yuba-Donner Byway

Nevada City and Grass Valley in the Northern Mines District on the State Highway 49 Golden Chain lead to The Yuba-Donner Scenic Byway on a loop from the junction of State Highway 20.

Donner Pass Monument at Alder Creek Valley, on the high plateau where Fall weather of 1846's unstoppable snowfall stranded the Donner Party.

NEVADA COUNTY WATER SPORTS

SOUTH YUBA – WASHINGTON TO EDWARDS CROSSING
This Class III and Class IV whitewater runs along a very accessible reach of the South Yuba River are characterized by gravel bars, bedrock and boulder gorges. Access from the bridge in Washington via Highway 20 north of Nevada City.

SOUTH YUBA – EDWARDS CROSSING TO PURDON CROSSING
This section of the South Yuba River is available only when river flows are whitewater at 350 cubic feet per second or more. The river is Class II and Class IV whitewater, used only by well-skilled groups. Access at Edwards Crossing on Tyler Road and North Bloomfield Road, north of Nevada City. Primitive campgrounds are offered on a first come, first serve basis.

BLAIR LAKE
This lake in Malakoff Diggins State Park provides swimming from July through September. Access via North Bloomfield Rd., north of Nevada City or Tyler Foote Crossing, east of North San Juan.

ENGLEBRIGHT RESERVOIR
Access off Highway 20 west of Grass Valley on Mooney Flat Road, offering waterskiing, fishing and most types of water recreation. Houseboat rentals are available, and a private marina is operational. Near the western boundary of Nevada County stocked with rainbow trout, also brown trout. Warm-water fish include largemouth and smallmouth bass, channel catfish and bluegills.

JACKSON MEADOWS
Access to camping, boating, swimming, fishing, hiking and biking. The dirt road connects to Sierra City near Highway 89, west of Truckee. Fingerling trout are planted. Brown trout up to 14 pounds have been caught. Lake of the Woods is for those seeking large brown trout as well as rainbows. Access to either lake from Henness Pass Road. East of Truckee from Sierra City off Highway 89.

Bullards Bar Reservoir on the Yuba River North Fork, along Highway 49.

BOCA, BOWMAN LAKE
Wildlife area with campsites, swimming, fishing, small lakes and boating, off Highway 89, or Tyler Foote Road. A rough but passable road for camping, boating, swimming, fishing, hiking and biking. Lakes and creeks with rainbow, brown and redband trout. Fuller Lake is planted with rainbow trout and good for bank fishing; Blue Lake, for fingerling rainbows and browns; and Fordyce Creek carries small numbers of natural rainbow and brook trout. Bowman Lake Road, from Highway 20 east of Nevada City.

SCOTTS FLAT RESERVOIR
Boating, Swimming, Fishing. Boat rentals are available, with a concrete boat launching ramp, and a marina in operation. Rainbow, brown trout, smallmouth, largemouth bass and Kokanee. Complete boat-launching facilities. Access off Highway 20 east of Nevada City.

BULLARDS BAR RESERVOIR
Bullards is accessed from Highway 49 north of Nevada City, turn west on Marysville Road, or Moonshine Rd. The reservoir extends 16 miles along the Yuba River North Fork with 56 miles of shoreline, stocked with McCourtney rainbow trout and Kokanee, a landlocked Sockeye salmon. Warm-water species include bass, catfish and sunfish.

ROLLINS RESERVOIR
Rollins Lake offers waterskiing, fishing and most types of water recreation. It is an 800-acre lake east of Nevada City and Grass Valley, with boat ramps, and stocked with rainbow, brown trout, largemouth, smallmouth bass, also very large catfish and smaller warm-eater varieties including bluegills and sunfish. Access from Highway 174, between Grass Valley and Colfax.

LAKE SPAULDING
Boat launching and swimming are available at this lake and nearby Lake Fuller. Access from Highway 20 near the intersection of Interstate 80.

Swimming Spots

Kelcher and Golden Quartz picnic areas. The South Yuba River provides swimming, seasonally July through September. Both picnic areas are upstream on the South Yuba at Washington, by crossing the bridge on the north side of Washington, and turning right.

Rollins Lake Campground.

Nevada County Sports

Steephollow

An eight-mile cross country ski trail with difficulty from easy to moderate, reaches elevations of nearly 5,000 feet. The trailhead begins at Alpha Omega Rest Stop, 17-miles east of Nevada City on State Highway 20's north side. Trails extend from the Omega Rest area to the Lake Spaulding Overlook.

Nyack Emigrant Gap Sno-Park

Marked cross-country ski trails and snowmobile tours are available. Access at the Nyack Rd. Exit 156 on Interstate 80.

Cisco Grove Sno-Park

Snowmobile trails. Also available is a small snow play area. Access from the Cisco Grove Exit 165 on Interstate 80.

Big Bend

Snow play, cross country skiing and snowmobiling. Trails aren't marked. Use Cisco Grove and Soda Springs topographic maps for reference. Easy to moderately difficult, elevations from 5,700 feet to 7,000 feet. Access from Big Bend Exit 166 off Interstate 80, and the trailhead is approximately a half-mile from the exit on Hampshire Rocks Road.

Donner Lake

Sno-Park at Donner Lake has marked ski trails to Donner Lake and Donner Party Historic Sites. No sledding or snowmobiles. Donner Lake Piers provide boat launching facilities. Mackinaw trout and Rainbow trout are planted each year for anglers. Access west of Truckee at the Donner Lake Exit from Interstate 80, and Donner Pass Road south of the freeway.

A Gold Country sculpture by Dr. Kenneth Fox.

Historical Nevada City's colorful downtown is the perfect background on special days.

Gold Rush mining display, in downtown Nevada City.

Prosser OHV Trailhead

Numerous unmarked routes for snowmobilers going through the Prosser Hill area. Gently rolling, at 6,000 feet on approximately nine-miles of trails with outstanding views. Access is off Highway 89, four-miles north of Truckee.

Truckee

Historic district, with access from I-80 near many high elevation ski areas, several older buildings house restaurants, shopping, and activity areas downtown. Access to Lake Tahoe's north shore is 14.6 miles and 34 miles to Reno, NV. The Truckee Legacy Regional Park and bike trailhead is a 6-mile trek along the Truckee River. Local historical spots include the Emigrant Trail Museum, Donner Lake, Donner Memorial State Park, and Donner Lake Rim Trail with stunning views accessed from Castle Peak, off I-80.

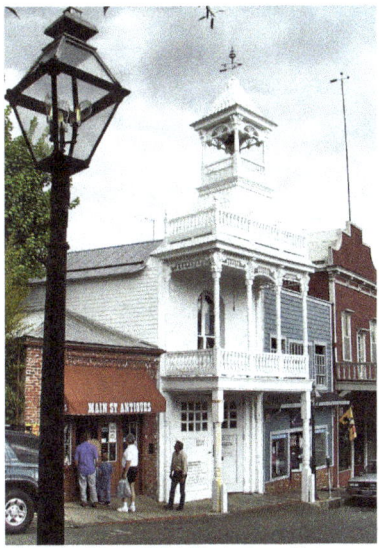
Nevada City's 1861 Firehouse #1.

Old Nevada Theatre on Broad St. dates to 1865 and once featured Mark Twain.

DOWNHILL SKIING AT DONNER SUMMIT
Boreal is for beginners, intermediate, and advanced with two triple-chair lifts, seven double-chair, and one quad lift. Sugar Bowl at Norden has four double chairs, one gondola, one access chair, and two quad chair lifts. Tahoe Donner Downhill Ski Resort, Squaw Valley, Alpine Meadows, Palisades Tahoe are highly recommended. Northstar Ski Resort has expanded into a complex of ski and resort lodging accessible from State Highway 67, from I-80 in Truckee.

The downtown Truckee Railroad Station is the central Welcome Center of the area.

TOUR 9
SIERRA AND PLUMAS COUNTIES
GOLD LAKES BASIN & SIERRA VALLEY

Downieville's downtown Main Street on Highway 49.

DOWNIEVILLE GETAWAY

Visitors to Downieville enjoy a classic Gold Rush community and partake within the limitless recreational surroundings of water and healthy air. The town's Community Heritage Park lies on the river's edge with boardwalks downtown leading visitors past the earliest buildings of 1852, including the Sierra County Museum from an early architectual style of flat stones laid horizontally as walls outfitted with iron doors and shutters. The Mountain Messenger Building from 1853 has consistently housed the authentic historical Gold Rush newspaper published continuously from its beginning day. Other historical buildings in town include the Downieville Foundry & Machine Shop from 1855, the large corner brick Craycroft Building of 1850, also St. Charles Place with Costa's Grocery Store on Main Street. It's where old timers customarily gathered under the shady locust trees. The town remains much like during the Gold Rush with many of the same buildings lining the streets on raised wooden walkways.

One sad day, a grim gallows erected in 1857 behind the Courthouse was a scene of lynching the only woman in the Gold Country. On July 5th, 1851 the Fourth of July celebrations had riled up throngs of miners after uproarious events and bouts of drinking the day before. A man was found dead during the early morning hours, an Australian named Jack Cannon, and as the story is told, Jack, making his usual celebratory rounds on the Fourth suddenly landed inside the shanty of Juanita, her man beside her. The following morning visibly 'unsobered', he returned defiantly at her tent, and Juanita incensed with anger reportedly stabbing the man dead with her Bowie Knife warding off his advances. Town vigilantes demanded justice, then grouping up to make a short

Northern Gold Country

The St. Charles Place, hotel, bar and restaurant in the Craycroft building from 1852.

trial of it, within hours pronounced her guilty. As the inebriated miners joined with a mob cheering the dramatic hanging of Juanita within two hours, she maintained her dignity to the end. The surrounding frenzy included thousands observing the gruesome horror at the river crossing, and a dark tragedy in California Gold Rush history.

SIERRA CITY

Sierra City is perhaps the most picturesque mining center along the Golden Chain as the Highway 49 trail follows close to the edge of the Yuba River North Fork River at an elevation of 4,000 feet. The highway is overshadowed by a canopy of the immense mountainous Sierra Buttes towering majestically over the town, rising to the 8,000-foot level. The town became an early trading post after placer gold was discovered in 1850. A rain storm partially revealed a 103-pound nugget named the 'Monumental' in 1869 at the Sierra Buttes Mine and created great exhilaration for hardrock mining. The quaint town has many historic brick and stone structures and offers wonderful resort accommodations.

Upon completion of the building known as Busch & Herringlake on Main St., a local fraternal drinking order E Clampus Vitus celebrated the completion in the 1870s with their inscription above the door sill. The three-story brick building opened with the bottom floor occupied by general merchandise, the second floor as a restaurant, and the third floor serving as a community hall, set with a

The Downieville River Inn and Resort.

The town's original three-story brick building from 1871, an old Wells Fargo Office and largest structure in Sierra City was known as Busch & Herringlake.

spring-loaded dance floor. Sierra City's old Masonic Hall on State Highway 49 was built in 1863, the Zerloff Hotel in 1885, and the nearby 1850s cemetery and Fire Tower remain in the center of town. Due north, the historic landmark Kentucky Mine Stamp Mill & Museum is visible one mile from Sierra City, and the Bassett House of 1871, at the corner of Gold Lake Road and junction at Highway 49 leads into Gold Lakes Basin and its 50 wilderness lakes. The Pacific Crest Trail traverses over the lofty terrain of the Sierra Buttes, and near the summit are roads accessing the top either from Gold Lake Highway, or on the Round Lake Loop.

Yuba River North Fork, in Sierra County.

KENTUCKY MINE STAMP MILL & MUSEUM

Sierra County Historical Park & Museum located at the Kentucky Mine, is situated in the heart of Sierra County Gold Country at 100 Kentucky Mine Road, in Sierra City along Highway 49. Kentucky Consolidated Gold Mining Company was formed in 1853 and operated for one hundred years. Hardrock mining necessitated the construction of a large Stamp Mill in the 1860s, running on waterpower and flat-belting. The 10-Stamp Mill 1,000-pound stamps crushed gold-veined quartz ore. There's a small admission charge supporting the facility, and children 12 and under are free of charge. Picnic facilities are available.

The Sierra Buttes at 8,590 ft. elevation. is the prominent landmark of Sierra City rising across a 50-mile canyon.

An important Sierra County historical landmark from 1853, the Kentucky Mine Stamp Mill with its Museum tours features a working stamp mill with 1,000 lb. hammers and supports an outdoor public amphitheater on the hillside and presents their Summer Concert Series. The Park and Museum are open Memorial Day through September, Wednesday–Sunday, 10AM–5PM, weekends weather permitting. www.sierracountyhistory.org, call 530-862-1310.

The Kentucky Mine Museum Stampmill, in Sierra City.

SIERRAVILLE

In Sierraville, Sierra Hot Springs has been a popular destination retreat established during the 1850s. A walking trail or relaxing moment may be found there within a spectacular 700-acre setting for bird watching and listening, camping, lodging, and hot springs therapy. The two-story historic lodge was built in the 1870s by Sheriff Jack Campbell and still greets guests to a rustic inviting atmosphere, with 10 rooms and shared baths down the hall. Centered in downtown one mile from the hot springs the Globe Hotel, a sister property is fully-restored with 10 rooms furnished in antiques and a quiet comfortable setting. Less than an hour's drive are Reno Nevada, Tahoe Ski areas, luxury resorts, numerous lakes, rivers, with the wilderness areas of Sierra and Plumas County nearby via Highway 89 and 49.

An historic home from the 1870s in Sierraville, settled as Campbell, today is the Sierra Hot Springs resort.

GOODYEARS BAR

Goodyear's Creek spills into the North Fork of the Yuba's icy cold waters. A party of prospectors led by Andrew and Miles Goodyear in 1849 discovered the landmark on the river. After most of the party left to strike further north at Camp Downie, the Goodyears stayed and began making lucrative strikes along the river banks. By 1852, the camp was lined with "a goodly assortment of store-tents, miners' boarding cottages, and saloons," according to an early account. The old Pioneer Hotel remained as one of a dozen or so, built when the camp reached its heyday. There was a Chinatown attended by migrants and were often disdained by 49ers seeing them working the earlier mined diggings and obtaining the rewards of finding hidden placers after long hours of patient and laborious toil.

Sierra County offers abundant photographic opportunities, as here in Sierraville traveling on Highway 49.

A rare full-color panoramic view of Old Downieville from over hundred years ago.

Bassett's Station

Bassett's Station and Gold Lake Rd. is five miles north of Sierra City on Highway 49. Bassett House, from 1871, is located on the way to the Gold Lakes Basin at Gold Lake Road with over 50 lakes.

Gold Lake Resorts

The largest lake in Sierra County is Gold Lake approached from Gold Lake Road, also leading further towards other lakes and trails. In both Plumas and Tahoe National Forests, intersected by the forks of the Feather River, Gold Lake in Sierra County lies over the line of Plumas County, where a second smaller Gold Lake lies northwest at Spanish Peak. From Highway 49 at Bassett's Station, take Gold Lake Highway north and access Salmon Lake, Packer Lake, Sardine Lakes, Big Bear Lake, Goose Lake, Haven Lake, Snag Lake, Frazier Falls, and other recreational destinations. Salmon Lakes with two popular well-stocked fishing lakes includes a wharf and boat launch. Gold Lake was once a 'fabled' discovery described by one man's story of gold-pebbled shores. Leading 1000 men into the Sierra region his predictions never materialized. Chiseled Sierra canyons 2,000 feet deep flank the lofty forested ridges and green fertile alpine valleys with countless streams nestled among hills by the mirrored-beauty of numerous lakes. The valleys between them include Indian, American, Big Meadows, Buck's, Humbug, Mohawk, Genesee, Sierra, Beckwourth, Long, Red Clover, Round, Last Chance, Onion, and others. Gold

View from Highway 49 of the Bassetts Station in Sierra County, a popular layover for gas, supplies, and campers in the area.

Sierra County's Gold Lake Basin offers campsites, fishing, and boating at 50 lakes.

Lake Basin is a major fly fishing area along the Scenic and Wild Middle Fork of the Feather River near Highway 89. 50 glacial lakes at 5,000-6,000 foot elevations are packed with trout, many with boat ramps, water skiing, kayaking, windsurfing, wildlife viewing, hiking, swimming, horseback riding and camping. Named in 1850, Gold Lake is the largest lake in Sierra County located between the North Fork of the Yuba River and the South Fork of the Feather River from Highway 49. Sierra County trails also connect to the Pacific Crest Trail on over a 2,000-mile journey between Canada and Mexico. Gold Lake Pack Station, 530-836-0940.

Loyalton

A historical area settled in the 1850s once called Smithneck due to the Smith Mining Company and with the outbreak of the Civil War became Loyalton, in 1863. Today it's the largest town known as a cattle and lumber center. The Milton Gottardi Museum, a former schoolhouse includes an auditorium and exhibits of railroading, logging, native and local memoriablia from around the Sierra Valley. Loyalton City Park is open May–Oct 30, Thurs–Sun, 1-5PM., 530-993-6750

Over 100-years old, this panorama taken in Sierra County of Forest City at a serene 4,500-foot elevation near Highway 49, reveals mine tailings in the foreground.

Forest City
Eight miles southeast of Downieville, Forest City was a lively camp of the mid-1850s, adopting its name from a woman resident and early settler to the surrounding conifer forests, Mrs. Forest Mooney, a newspaper correspondent. On the opposite side of the canyon where miners struck paydirt in 1855 at the Allegheny Tunnel and the entire town evacuated to the new camp, leaving the original Forest behind in shambles.

Sattley
Located at the eastern slope of the Sierra, Sattley offers a view of early ranching and logging. The Turner Barn visible from the road is well over a century old.

Recreational Spots
Indian Rock Picnic Area
Native people have used this area for at least 4,000 years, on Highway 49 between Indian Valley and Goodyear's Bar, at a stop allowing public access to the Yuba River's North Fork for swimming, camping and fishing.

Sierra Buttes Recreation Area
Located in the Tahoe National Forest with hiking along the Pacific Crest Trail with numerous lakes and streams, fishing, well-marked horseback trails, snowmobiling and cross country skiing within spectacular mountain country. The Buttes fire lookout is a spectacular mountain hike accessible via Gold Lake Road and from Packer Lake, left on County 621 to Packer Pocket up the steep grade, left on Butcher Ranch Road, and a half-mile to trailhead parking marked for the Buttes. Hike a 2.3 miles on a rise of 1,587 feet in elevation following one-mile along the Pacific Coast Trail to the top. The Sierra Buttes highest elevation is 8,591 feet and the metal staircase built by forestry in 1964 provides safety to the public for access of the incredible views at one of the most visited Sierra landmark destinations.

Lakes Basin Region Fishing & Camping
700 miles of well-stocked streams in a 45-mile area of high lakes. Elwell Lakes, Gold Lake, Packer Lake, Salmon and Sardine Lakes have lodging, camping and RV parking.

SIERRA COUNTY HISTORICAL SPOTS

View of the Sierra Valley near Beckwourth Pass, from Highway 49.

THE SIXTEEN TO ONE MINE

The Whopper

High in the Sierra, a road trip is rewarded with an adventure of a lifetime in visiting the Alleghany back country and going underground nearly one-quarter mile into the depths of the Original Sixteen to One Mine. Located at 4,300 feet elevation on Pliocene Ridge, the Original-Sixteen-to-One has been in operation for over a century with nearly 27 miles of tunnels. Alleghany is a Gold Rush town having one foot in the past and one in the future – a place where one gets an early sense of history fostering the renewal possible by modern technology. Alleghany reflects a rich heritage of over a century of continuous mining. Many of the historic buildings still standing are an assurance of their preservation. Sharing and preserving faith in the gold miners, the new history of this mining town conveys an excitement as one of America's few working gold mines once the vision developed in today's Alleghany Underground Gold Miners Museum. A one-time livery stable, the museum features exhibits about the evolution of drilling technology, a photographic history of gold mining, cable technology with displays leading to the invention of the ski lift, and video footage. The museum sponsors tours for visitors of the Original Sixteen to One Mine, the historic shop buildings, trails, and earliest-working part of the mine at the 250-foot level with the original mine portal. Tours by actual miners underground explain the mining and milling process. "Underground mining, more than anything I know, tests all of man's capabilities and powers. It requires a combination of brute strength and intelligence, of instinct and knowledge, each one as important as the other," relates Original Sixteen to One Mine President, Michael Miller," and it is this paradox that gives us our passion for working

Highway 49 and Sierra Buttes in Sierra City.

underground and lures us back day after day like the song of the sirens." Even under the current operating portal at the 800 ft. level, the tour leads underground to the hoist room and the 'Ballroom' at the 1,100 ft. level. Here the miner familiarizes guests with the legends of Tommyknockers, or spirits of miners who knock on beams to warn present-day miners of possible cave-ins, ghosts, and superstitions. The tour also passes near the 'stope' where the treasures of the 1993 'Million Dollar Day' were found. "In times of global uncertainty and the high rate of change, gold mining becomes increasingly attractive," continues Miller. "Most gold production comes from distant mines as far away as South America, Indonesia, Africa, etc. and progress only tracked on paper. The Original Sixteen to One Mine is right here in California and people can come up and 'kick the tires," adds Miller. "Great leaders, great events, and great loves have been immortalized in gold, and our quest for high-grade gold is more than a dream. It is a mindset and way of life. Underground mining captures the spirit of the Old West and thrusts us into the unknown future." Metal detectors, ground penetrating radar, and computer analysis can aid today's miners, but he still shares the basic attributes of his 19th-century counterparts; the faith to live and work in the hope of finding and following the next rich vein. Museum and tours call, 530-287-3330

PLUMAS COUNTY — SIERRA VALLEY

BECKWOURTH PASS

Jim Beckwourth was a trapper living for a time in Colorado as scout and honorary Crow Indian chief, however he was born in Virginia enslaved, in 1798. Coming to California in 1850, discovering a mountain pass with his party, the trail was first used as the crossing from the American River Valley to Pit River Valley. The trail is today's Highway 70 near Vinton, and was the popular miner's path from Marysville and the Sacramento Valley. Beckwourth settled Sierra Valley, the largest sub-alpine valley in the country, geographically formed by an ancient lake bed during the Ice Age. The historic Beckwourth cabin was the Trading Post store, historic inn, and ranch house.

Historic Sierra Valley outlook, Hwy 49.

Gold Rush Contemporary
James "Jim" Beckwourth

Fur Trader, Mountain Man and Honorary Chief of the Crow Indians

Born into slavery in Virginia, Jim Beckwourth was the first settler near the Feather River in the Sierra Valley, and lived in his handmade cabin that today is a museum and monument to him. Serving as a guide for multitudes of wagon trains and ox-drawn schooners, and helping settlers to the Golden State, he discovered the pass during a prospecting expedition as a trapper and trail scout in 1851, not far from the present day town of Beckwourth, between the American River and Pit River Valleys. Beckwourth built the first cabin and was first to settle the expansive alpine Sierra Valley plateau establishing a trading post. He proposed a wagon trail transiting the Feather River Canyon from Marysville into the Sierra, serving travelers as a better route than from nearby Truckee and Donner Pass. It became a well trodden path of emigrants to the Sierra goldfields in the 1850s, as well as the silver mines of Virginia City of Nevada, just ten years later. Also, the area was chosen for establishing the northern pass of the Western Pacific Railway.

Jim Beckwourth

One of his first passengers, Ina Coolbirth, at age 11 was destined to become the first poet-laureate of California and described Beckwourth as an historic figure. "He wore his hair in two long braids, twisted with colored cord giving him a picturesque appearance…he wore a leather coat and moccasins and rode a horse without a saddle." After three days journey with the family into the Sierra, Beckwourth was quoted to say, "Here is California, little girls, here is your kingdom."

The Beckwourth Cabin built in 1851, remains a museum, honoring the pioneer settlement.

The Sierra Valley is the largest open sub-alpine valley in the nation. The Beckwourth Pass served miners of the 1849 California Gold Rush and the Nevada Comstock Lode.

JOHNSVILLE

The owners of the Plumas-Eureka Mine began with a combination of miners from 1851 who joined into one company-owned town, lasting until 1943 with estimates running as high as $20,000,000 in gold ore production. It is a part of Plumas County records dating back to 1860, when it's referred to men of the town using a down-the-hill ski run of 2,600 feet and race up to 90 miles an hour at the oldest recorded sport skiing spot in the western hemisphere. History explains that mining ore buckets on Gold Mountain were used by skiers possibly as the first ever ski-lift in the world. In 1937, two men from Quincy designed the first ski lift at Mt. Washington in New Hampshire, then removing it after an avalanche and moved it to Plumas County to the steep slopes behind the Plumas-Eureka Mine Stamp Mill. The present-day park museum served once as a ski lodge. Little Grass Valley Lake is a destination in the Plumas National Forest with 323 campsites. The impound of water from the Feather River's South Fork and several streams feed the lake stocked annually with rainbow trout. The Lakeshore Trail provides hiking, mountain biking, fishing, and equestrian opportunities.

LA PORTE

Once settled as Rabbit Creek from 1850-1857, later named La Porte at the southwest corner of Plumas County, the 2010 census counted 26 residents. During the peak of the Gold Rush, the town supported four large hotels, five gambling houses, 14 saloons, 15 stores and two churches. It's the mining town where Lotta Crabtree spent her early childhood. A hub to fifty mining companies operating in 1857, hydraulic mining had yielded up to $4,000,000 a year, in decreasing amounts over the next 10 years. A resurgence in mining there in the 1890s brought new machinery and mining techniques to the area.

Blairsden - Graeagle

Along State Highway 89 and Highway 70, north of Sierra County's Gold Lakes Basin, both Graeagle and Blairsden offer countryside golfing resorts and museums including the Williams House, Jim Beckwourth Museum and Cabin, Western Pacific Railroad Museum, and Plumas County Museum.

Portola

Adventures await both seeing the collection and riding the Western Pacific Railroad Museum trains, the largest diesel engine museum of its kind. On display are many engines from the Western Pacific Railway, once the transcontinental link across the country near the Feather River Canyon.

Rich Bar

The stragglers from the Gold Lake group on the way to seeking gold strayed here and discovered one of the foremost mines in Plumas County, during July of 1850. Located on a branch of the Feather River North Fork, a tremendous find made panning production equaling $100 to $1000 per scoop from the river's gravel bar. Three German miners earned $36,000 in four days from nuggets and gold dust there, and it was so rich that limits were imposed to 10 square feet per claim. During the first two years, Rich Bar yielded up to $4,000,000, implying its name. Pioneer accounts spoke of the hotel called the 'Empire' that was given the name 'Hotel', being the only hostelry in town with a bar-room fitted at the center with an elegant mirror setting off a background of decanters, cigar vases, and jars of brandied fruit. The entire building was lined with calico purple alternated by a delicate blue, as described by the pioneer wife, Mrs. Clappe, during her days witnessing the Gold Rush there. "That eternal crimson calico of the bar…flushes the whole social life of the 'Golden State' with its everlasting red, and the effect is really quite pretty. The floors are so uneven that you are always ascending a hill or descending into a valley." The one-time gambler's palace cost its original owners more than $8,000 to build, way out in the far reaches of the Sierra hills.

A giant Sierra snowplow, Portola Railroad Museum.

Northern Gold Country

A view towards the Yuba River North Fork Canyon in the Sierra Foothills on Highway 49, near Gold Lake Road.

GREENVILLE

A center of quartz mining activity, Greenville was settled in 1851, and first profitably mined by John W. Ellis in 1856. He opened Ellis Mine in 1862 with a stamp mill, and a large village grew up around it. The town faded immediately after a few years. To the southeast, the Crescent Mills quartz mining and milling operations had carried on through 1926.

HIGHWAY 49'S NORTHERN TERMINUS

Completing the Gold Rush journey on Highway 49 at an elevation of nearly 5,000 feet, from its beginning at the southern-end of Yosemite National Park to its northernmost tip, the old miner's trail reaches its terminus in Vinton, at State Highway 70. The final mile of State Highway 49 lies in view of the expansive grazing areas of Sierra Valley, in Plumas County.

Gold Rush Historic Parks
Plumas-Eureka State Historic Park
310 Johnsville Rd, Blairsden, CA 96103

The Old Mohawk 80-stamp mill at Plumas-Eureka Mine was constructed in 1878. 530-836-2380

Enjoy the view along the State Highway 49 Golden Chain and visit the Plumas-Eureka Mine, 150 miles from Sacramento and 80 miles from Lake Tahoe. The Plumas-Eureka Mine Gold Rush State Historic Park lies along the eastern slope of the Sierra Nevada Range at the Sierra Valley plateau, over 5,000-feet in elevation. Migrant prospectors had not found their way up to Plumas-Eureka until a large group discovered an exposed quartz mineral-rich ledge with gold, perched high on the Eureka Peak slopes. 36 miners joined the Eureka Company and the rush began. Another 76 claimants formed the Washington Company known as the Seventy-Six. Another 40 miners claimed the Rough-and-Ready digs, and about 80 additional claims were filed for the Mammoth, first using crude arrastras-stones dragged by mules for crushing quartz into lode-bearing ore. The introduction of a 12-stamp mill installed in 1856 contributed to the profitable yields lasting through 1870. The early mines were sold in the 1870s to the Sierra Buttes Company of London. Today, the mines have grown over with brush where the road used by oxen-drawn wagons hauled loads of aggregate down from the summit of Eureka Hill. During its heyday, the 80-stamp mill increased total production to nearly $20,000,000. In 1876, Johnstown, established at Jamison Creek and one-half mile from the Plumas-Eureka mine, processed gold from the Plumas-Eureka area hard rock at the Mohawk Stamp Mill. Compared to panning for placer gold nuggets, the early underground mining explorations here after 1852 became the more profitable method of mining gold. A recent census counted 20 people living there in modern times. The rural mountain roads in Plumas County leave visitors the reward of the best fall foliage in all of California, with diverse species of trees such as the California black oak, big leaf maple, quaking aspen, and black cottonwood. Favorite spots include the nearby Feather River Canyon, Lake Almanor, Indian Valley, the Quincy-Oroville Road, the Quincy-La Porte Road, Round Valley Reservoir Road, and Gold Lakes Basin.

Northern Gold Country 131

An isolated pioneer foothill mining town in Sierra County near the Yuba River North Fork.

The Western Pacific Railroad Museum in Portola, Plumas County, founded in 1983, currently offers train rides on weekends.

Plumas-Eureka Mine Historic Gold Rush Park and Mohawk Stamp Mill, in Johnsville and the Northern Mines.

Between Pine Grove and Pioneer, Chaw'se Grinding Rock State Historic Park is a traditional center of the Gold Country Native Miwok over centuries. The park is near the Central Region mining towns of Amador County and holds an annual Pow Wow each mid-April, lasting overnight.

East of Jackson, the massive historical native grinding rock mortars remain intact across the park, across from the native traditional roundhouse. The name of the site is "Chaw'se", or the Miwok word for "grinding rock".

133

III. Central Gold Country

TOUR 10
Amador Mining & Agriculture

State Highway 16 from Sacramento follows a 42-mile drive into the Central Gold Country and passes Sloughhouse towards Plymouth, joining Highway 49 at the gateway of the Shenandoah Valley's lush foothill vineyards. Dozens of wineries line the valley's floor, within the Amador Appellation of rich loamy soils producing the finely flavored, deep, dark, delicious Old Vine Zinfandel and lighter Chablis-style vintage wines. Amador County's gateway meanders past streams on the Golden Chain of Highway 49, where open placer mining created wealth in the early mining towns of Drytown, Amador City, Sutter Creek and Jackson in the Mother Lode. Colorful Gold Country side journeys include Old Fiddletown, Volcano, Martell, Pine Grove, Lake Camanche and Ione. An excursion north reveals many recreational features along Highway 88 passing Silver Lake, Caples Lake, Kirkwood to Carson Pass and Lake Tahoe.

State Highway 49, at Sutter Creek along the Golden Chain. Sutter Creek's Visitor Center for more information, 209-267-1344.

From Sutter's Fort, John A. Sutter traveled from Sacramento to this locality in 1848, looking for placer gold after he and James Marshall ignited gold fever that captivated thousands of early California settlers prospecting ventures throughout the Gold Country. The flow of the Sutter Creek watershed follows Eureka Street with frontage running into downtown. Later, miners at Sutter Creek explored underground beginning in 1851 for quartz gold producing lode ore at the Central Eureka Mine, the largest producer in all the Southern Mother Lode. Amador County mined more gold ore than any of the Central and Southern Mother Lode region's at many former mining camps and ghost towns. Within 12 miles, between Plymouth and the Middlebar, on the Mokelumne River sprung up more than 45 mines operating at once including the famous Kennedy and Argonaut, with each producing nearly half the gold mined in the region. During the Gold Rush, Amador County production

There are parades every July 4th throughout California Gold Country streets commemorating the years of the Gold Rush and celebrating our Country's independence. (Ray Moore)

Downtown Sutter Creek on Highway 49. The mines of Amador County exceeded all others regions in the immediate production of gold during the Gold Rush.

exceeded more than any other county in the Mother Lode's southern region for gold and home to eight mining camps, most running roughly north-to-south over what we know as State Highway 49. Significant wealth flowed through the area at what were mining camps evolved into bustling communities, well-preserved and enjoyed today for their historical ambiance. One of the most picturesque is Sutter Creek, located in the middle of the county on Highway 49, and

An 1880s brick stone mix building in Plymouth on Main St., formerly Ming's Chinese Store.

described by Sunset magazine in 2004 "as the best place in California to live."

Plymouth

A significant northern town crossroads in the Central Gold Country once named Puckerville, is still referred to its nickname of Pokerville. Of several historical locations well worth a visit are lush vineyards of Shenandoah Valley. Plymouth initially developed by Alvinza Hayward who purchased interest in the Aden-Simpson – Plymouth Mine in 1859, had successes at Sutter Creek gold mines and the silver mines of the Comstock Lode. Hayward had created employment and the town expanded with hotels, saloons, stores, a post office in 1871, and thereafter naming the town Plymouth. Hayward's efforts producing $30,000-50,000 each month in gold, the mine sold in 1878 to a New York company including the mill and mining ditches for $2,000,000. The town suffered losses from fire in 1877, and quickly rebuilt the schools, churches and a racetrack.

In Drytown, this 1850's brick building was a mine office, print shop and antique store.

Drytown and Amador City

Established in 1848 and the oldest settlement in Amador County, Drytown was explored by Americans, Native Indians and Mexican gold seekers for its rich gravel beds and brought legendary tales of raucous miners heard celebrating $100 days panning nearby streams. The names used were Rattlesnake Gulch, Murderer's Gulch, Mile Gulch, Forest Home, Arkansas Creek, Willow Springs and Yankee Hill. Drytown boasted 26 saloons and nearly all were consumed by fire in 1857. Today, historical spots include a centuries-old adobe house in the town dating back to the early mission period. On State Highway 49, two Gold Rush buildings still are standing

J Monteverde General Merchant, Sutter Creek.

with one from 1871, the Drytown Schoolhouse and a Community Hall next door. Amador City, the smallest incorporated town in California, was settled in 1851, with landmarks visible from Highway 49. In their original state, 24 buildings remain standing in town on a walking tour through history. Perched above Highway 49's west side, the massive red brick Mine House was the headquarters for the Consolidated Keystone Mine from 1867.

SUTTER CREEK

Of the more picturesque foothill towns in the Gold Country on Highway 49 at the 1,200-foot elevation, a Sutter Creek walkabout through town passes over 60 historical places of interest. There are B&B inns, early hotels, restaurants, antique shops, local cultural events, and lively people within a thriving foothill center. John A. Sutter was the first miner in this locality during 1848. After the transition to quartz gold mining by 1851, initial crude mining tunnels constructed without understanding of safe timbering caused cave-ins and tragedies. Alvinza Hayward invested in buying out several mines, such as the Central Eureka Mine discovered in 1869, explored underground to the 2,300-foot level turning the mine into the best-paying of all the Southern Mother Lode, operating until 1932.

KNIGHT FOUNDRY ON EUREKA STREET

Around the corner on Highway 49 Sutter Street, the historical Knight Foundry buildings at 81 Eureka Street

At a casting pour at Knight Foundry's, an American national treasure, from 1873.

were established in 1873. It is the last water-powered foundry in use nationally. The foundry supplied heavy custom made cast iron tools and equipment, and was a well-known manufacturer of iron castings in the Mother Lode, and repair facility for the Gold Country gold mines and timber industry. The foundry is moving the tradition forward as a rare example of a water-operated machine shop, and over decades fabricating castings and industrial items while training apprentices, as in the old Gold Rush days.

Volcano

12 miles east of Sutter Creek is the unique Gold Rush town Volcano discovered in 1848 by Colonel Stevenson's Regiment, after an encampment made at the bottom of a deep cup in the mountains at Soldiers Gulch. Their earnings from placer mining piled up to $100 and as much as $500, each day. The town's name came from the unusual formation of the area, reminding miners of working inside a volcano crater, and the name stuck. After the winter's arrival, a small group of Stevenson's Regiment had remained camped during a fierce winter freeze with little permanent shelter. The soldiers succumbed to icy frostbite and were discovered months later. As swarms of prospectors arrived at the goldfields, by 1855 profiting from using powerful pressurized streams called 'hydraulicking' introduced visible destructive damage. An old Stone Brewery opened downtown Volcano in 1856. The enormity of gold enterprises brought thousands of fortune seekers into the town which grew to 17 hotels and added a library, theater and courts of justice. Volcano productivity created $90,000,000 of gold ore, much of that value for financing the Union during the Civil War. Miners who were Southern sympathizers threatened to reroute the local bullion to the South, and in response the 'Volcano Blues' were formed. The story of a smuggled cannon 'Old Abe' brought there hidden during the dead of night in a hearse and later let loose with a few loud blasts to quell the Rebel neighbors in the area. Today, cultural flavor of performances by the Volcano Theatre Co. and the Cobblestone Theatre offer productions each season. Recognized on the National Historic Registry, Volcano's St. George Hotel built in 1862 as the tallest, most elegant Mother Lode hotel.

Volcano's Cobblestone Theatre is held outdoors behind the facade of the Clute Building, from 1855.

Sutter Creek on State Highway 49's Golden Chain leads to the Central and Southern Mines of the Mother Lode, from the 1849 Gold Rush.

Jackson
The Louisiana House and National Hotel

From the corner of Main and Water Street, Jackson's National Hotel rises three stories well above all others, overlooking downtown Jackson. At the rear, Bottilleas Spring, the original panning site once explored by the town's earliest founders remains a landmark along the original road between Sacramento and the Mokelumne River. The National Hotel, considered today's second most authentic site settled in Jackson, was developed by Ellis Evans in 1850 as a butcher shop. He and partners, D.C. White and Armstrong Askey, built a two-story wooden hotel building named the Louisiana House, but after the structure burned down in a town fire of 1862, in the Spring of 1863, a new brick hostelry renamed the National Hotel began as a large two-story, later expanded to three stories. Of the Gold Country's present-day lodges, there are three similar 'National Hotel' inns, one in the Northern Mines of Nevada City with another in Jamestown. Each National Hotel is a highly rated authentic full-service historical lodge with full-service restaurants open daily.

Central Gold Country

Since 1879, the Imperial Hotel's imposing two-story brick structure opened as a Gold Country traditional Bed & Breakfast on State Highway 49, in Amador City.

A Mark Twain Commentary on the Gold Country

"You will find it hard to believe that once stood a fiercely flourishing little city of 2,000 or 3,000 souls, with its newspaper, fire company, brass band, volunteer militia, bank, hotels, noisy Fourth of July processions and speeches, gambling halls crammed with tobacco smoke, profanity, and rough bearded men of all nations and colors, with tables heaped with gold dust –its streets crowded and rife with business– town lots worth $400 each riverfront foot –labor, laughter, music, swearing, fighting, shooting, stabbing –a bloody inquest and a man for breakfast every morning –and now nothing but lifeless, homeless solitude left. In no other land, in modern times, have towns so absolutely died and disappeared, as in the old mining regions of California."

Downtown Sutter Creek on Highway 49.

Sutter Gold Mine

The Lincoln, Comet, and Keystone mines are historical hard rock enterprises located off Highway 49, on String Bean Alley just north of Amador City. The Lincoln Mine led Leland Stanford to make his fortune and enabled the founding of Stanford University, along with the Big Four partnership financing the Central Pacific Railroad. A modern Australian gold company, Seduli, presently operates the mines and predicts they could uncover much more of the original Mother Lode discovered from a potential of several million ounces left in the deep bedrock below. The up-to-date company plans employ automation in mining and today's leaders within their segment of the gold industry. The new aim is to mine exploratory drifts of gold over a three-mile region within an area of the Mother Lode famous for a higher grade of 23K ore, generally around a half-mile deep or more, at 13660 Highway 49.

Argonaut and Kennedy Mines

'Argonaut' is a term applied to Jason of the Golden Fleece from Homeric lore and used by two African American miners, James Hager and William Tudor, with the 1850 discovery of a mine just west of Highway 49 in Jackson. After the sale of the mine in 1860 and consolidation by the mining industry, the deep shaft with the mine eventually bored out to below 5,912 feet, the total ore produced at Argonaut Mine valued at $25,279,160, at the time of the mine's closing. In 1919, became the scene of horrific tragedies when disaster struck the Argonaut Mine and again in 1922, fires burning at the 3,000-foot level had overtaken 47 workers below the raging flames. A tunnel bored across at the Kennedy Mine attempted to make a rescue in reaching the burnt-out shaft but not in time to survive the fire's poisonous gases, smoke, and heat, in retrieval of the trapped miners.

Quartz mining was a main source of employment and in 1856, Andrew Kennedy, an Irish immigrant, located a quartz vein and combined the discovery with other claims, forming the highly productive Kennedy Mine. Kennedy Mine became among the largest Gold Country producers in the nation, adding upwards to $105,268,760 in mined gold bullion. The Kennedy Mine, descending 5,912 feet, competes as one of the deepest mines of the Gold Country. Although both mines closed in 1942, the Argonaut

A hillside 'Headframe' at the Argonaut Mine.

reopening continued past the 6,300-foot depth, and in 1938 brought $17,391,409 out in gold bullion. With a 60-stamp mill installed in 1942, a more novel introduction of a plunging wrecking ball raised productivity by over 90%. As the Gold Rush spread through Amador County, several mines called 'Argonaut' arose with discoveries.

In 1862, another threatening fire in Jackson was set by accident and destroyed most of the town in about three hours. One survivor, the Levy Brother Dry Goods Store, dates from 1854 at 38 Main Street. Another, the Republic House Hotel, was built in 1858 and remains at 104 Main Street. The building at 111-115 Main Street, the Native Daughters of the Golden West surviving the fire of 1862, occupies two buildings still combined in one, from 1855. Few buildings resurrected after the fires of the most original ones, including the courthouse with its records, were consumed.

St. Patrick's Church was rebuilt in 1869 on Church Street.

Hidden from sight to the rear of the Knight machine shop on Eureka Street are assortments of rusty projects and casting molds stored for later use.

Highway 49's trail of the Golden Chain connects to many mining towns of the Southern, Central, and Northern Mines, along the western slope of the Sierra Nevada Foothills.

The Amador County Museum building was built as a residence in 1853, by one of the town's earliest settlers. Besides housing displays on gold history of the county, the 15-room museum contains collections of early fashions, Chinese Americans and Native Americans and is open 10AM–4PM, Wed-Sun. The museum can be reached at 209-223-6386.

A two-story brick home from 1859, once owned by Amstead Calvin Brown at 225 Church Street in Jackson, houses today's Amador County Museum.

The Keyes building's unique brick and rock exterior on Highway 49 displays colorful broadside advertisements. Today, it serves as the Sutter Creek Visitor Center.

BLACK CHASM CAVERN
NATIONAL HISTORICAL LANDMARK

A mile or two from Volcano, Black Chasm Cavern makes the most excellent underground diversion possible. Discovered by Gold Rush miners during a hair-raising descent into the cave, Black Chasm had few visits in the past but recently opened for public tours. The cave was named a National Natural Landmark in 1976 by the National Park Service, citing its outstanding geological significance. In particular, masses of helictite crystals in several areas of the noteworthy Landmark Room are unlike stalactites and stalagmites with formations not created by dripping water leaving calcite deposits, but from water under pressure pushing through tiny holes in the rock walls. Delicate, six-sided calcite crystals deposit haphazardly twisted out from the walls seemingly defying gravity and look like cooked spaghetti growing sideways out of the walls. These formations are very rare with the ones on display at Black Chasm quite incredible.

The Amador Hotel in Amador City, the smallest incorporated town in California.

FIDDLETOWN

First settled in 1849, a party of Missourians aptly named the town for settlers heard 'always fiddling'. The town's picturesque name was immortalized in Bret Harte's story, "An Episode of Fiddletown." A venerable herbal store, Chew Kee is a rammed-earth structure built in the 1850s by the Chinese settlers and stands downtown as it did during the Gold Rush remaining intact as a museum of relics and artifacts.

IONE

Historical village buildings from a vintage era of downtown Ione were once called 'Bedbug' and also 'Freezeout.' The fertile Ione Valley is home to recreational areas, numerous homes, churches and stores. Nearby Lake Camanche provides a fish stocking program to bring in anglers, with or without a boat for year-round trout, catfish, black bass, crappie and perch fishing. Boat rentals, berthing, and boat ramps are available on either side of the lake featuring dots of man-made islands to land on. Anglers try out bottom fishing if they find trolling on the slow side, with stocked trout, boating, fishing, swimming, picnicking, hiking, equistrian and camping available.

Fiddlers and musicians performing at one of Fiddletown's live events.

LAKE CAMANCHE

A landmark, Lake Camanche was a town once named Limerick, then in 1849 renamed after a town in Iowa. The lake lies between Amador, Calaveras, and San Joaquin counties. The rich mines nearby were Cat Camp and Sand Hill, and the area's population peaked at 1,500 during the Gold Rush. Water brought through Lancha Plana, a town inundated in 1950, had richer returns from the hill and bluff mining than from the river. Also, the Mokelumne River Poverty Bar ditch yielded rich rewards and a mooring place for a flatboat ferry carrying miners from the north side to the Calaveras mines. In 1873, a conflagration by fire destroyed the Chinatown at Camanche.

PINE GROVE

Pine Grove has historic buildings, camping, and recreational choices in the foothills of Amador County. The Pine Grove Hotel, once a stage stop, is a scenic destination of the Gold Country. Chaw'se, the native name for the mortar holes created in limestone outcroppings, are at Indian Grinding Rock State Park, containing the single largest rock known, covered by 363 mortars. The Nun ge roundhouse was constructed recently at the site and used for Pow Wow meetings and religious activities. Camping, available year-round, is subject to closure during heavy snowfall. There are 135 acres of trails around the reconstructed village of the Northern Miwuk and the intriguing Chaw'se Regional Indian Museum. 14881 Pine Grove/Volcano Rd., Pine Grove, 209-296-7488. Hours: 11 AM-3 PM, Mon-Fri; and 10 AM-4 PM Sat-Sun.

West Point

A legend confirms Kit Carson named West Point after discovering today's Carson Pass on his way west while leading the second Frémont expedition. Near the south side of the Mokelumne River, Carson decided not to travel further and turned back. The road was windy in the Gold Rush days traveling from Volcano and later in its history helped transform the area from mining production into a lumber town.

The 1850s Chew Kee Store, Fiddletown.

Pioneer

The capital of cedar pencils and the first of several stages stops leading to El Dorado National Forest and the Highway 50 trail. Pioneer on State Highway 88 rises to a 5,000-foot elevation. Mace Meadows Golf Course, Railroad Flat, and Cook's Station, are stops on the way. Railroad Flat was a slow-producing mine but was a rail terminus during the Gold Rush serving the mines there.

Silver Lake

50 miles east of Jackson, and 45 miles south of Lake Tahoe, on Highway 88 at Silver Lake. The Kit Carson Lodge offers accommodations and recreational features, fine dining, a General Store and an Art Gallery.

Pardee Reservoir Recreation Area

Pardee Lake provides fishing, boating, swimming, bicycling, picnicking, riding, and camping. Warm water trout fishing is stocked weekly in season.

New Hogan Lake

In Valley Springs, New Hogan Lake has over 300,000 acre-feet of water and is three miles long by one mile, featuring a marina, water skiing, fishing, and a choice of primitive campsites, with 189 developed sites and 30 boat-in campsites. There is year-round fishing with stocked stripers, Chinook salmon, crappies, bluegill and others. The 'River of Skulls', a hiking trail located below the dam at the Monte Vista Recreation Area, is also the staging area for an eight-mile equestrian trail, for information, 209-772-1343.

The Railroad Flat monument.

KENNEDY MINE TAILING WHEELS COUNTY PARK
JACKSON GATE RD., MARTELL 209-223-1646

Along State Highway 49, south of Sutter Creek in Martell turn left on Jackson Gate Road at the historical Kennedy Mine Tailing Wheels Park. Part of the nearby Kennedy Mining & Milling Corporation visible in Jackson from Highway 49 was consolidated with several mines in 1886 reaching a 5,912-foot depth. As one of the richest, deepest mines in the world, in 1914, built in a series of four wooden tailing wheels constructed with redwood buckets were used to eliminate mine tailings and silt, lifting the waste and moving as much as 850 tons each day. Aggregate ore from the mine crushed first by a 100-stamp mill on the south slope of Humbug Hill was mixed as a slurry and sent downhill along a 1000-foot flume to the base of the four large 58-foot diameter handmade wooden wheels. Working in unison 24 hours a day at 15 revolutions per minute, the tailing wheels successfully lifted tailings impounding the waste to an uphill basin at Indian Gulch. The project offered reclaimation in response to anti-pollution laws supporting clean water resources flowing into California's agricultural valleys. The wheels ran continuously until their closure due to WWII in 1942. The two remaining iconic tailing wheels are near the Kennedy Mine headquarters with 1-1/2 hour surface tours available, March through October, weekends and holidays. For information visit, www.kennedygoldmine.com.

Central Gold Country

Golfers enjoy being in the rolling hills at many Sierra Foothill resorts along Highway 49.

A frontier broadside promoting the services of Wells Fargo Express gold transport express services.

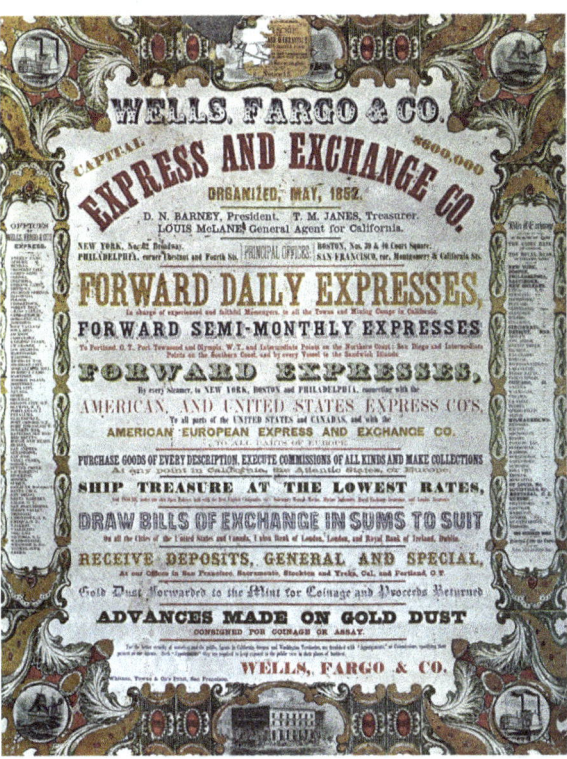

Gold Rush Contemporary
E.C.V. Historical Times, Places, and Personalities

Mark Twain's life during the 1860s as honored by E.C.V. art, Murphys, CA

Flourishing during the days of the Gold Rush, a fraternal drinking order formed under the name E Clampus Vitus was established around 1851. A somewhat spontaneous word was spread throughout Gold Country mining districts, and the order is still known in the Golden Chain's varied mining towns. A piece of Gold Country tradition, the order was revived in 1931, and well-respected and known for their community services, especially the ensconced bronze plaques historically honoring significant landmarks embedded into building fascia. The chapters commemorates noteworthy dates and persons on display at ghost towns, saloons, bordellos, ranchos, at times in honor of heroes or even an occasional madman. The strong system of Clampers' work involves cleaning buildings, fixing fences, creating monuments, even caring for the pine cone-strewn cemeteries of mining towns, or the repairing of disregarded wooden or marble century-old headstones. They gather help for those in need during a family member's loss, or by comforting victims of mining accidents. As agreed by each order's members, the 'Noble Grand Humbug' arises as the chapter's chief official head. Similar meetings occur throughout the Gold Country, and at E.V.C. commemorations, members may be seen with traditional red undershirts and suspenders. The steadfast E.C.V. Motto, 'Credo Quia Absurdum' from Latin translates roughly, "I believe because it's absurd". Calaveras County's town of Murphys erected a 'Wall of Comparative Ovations' outer wall at the Old Timer's Museum to feature a collection of intricately fashioned ceramic plaques on display. One honors Mark Twain and claims, "the droll behavior of contemporary Clampers appealed to his comic sense." E Clampus Vitus continues to celebrate as they did in Sierra County as on the completion in the 1870s of the Busch building, by honoring many of California's mining town's places of interest. In Plumas County's Club at Quincy, the Las Plumas Del Oro Chapter meetings are illuminated by a neon E.C.V. sign warmly lighting up the window both in the bar room and outside. There is a plaque commemorating the bar's opening in 1914, describing the saloon as a one-time dairy store with slot machines during Prohibition years. The bar's cork board 'Wall of Comparative Humbugery' displays odd and inconsequential memorabilia. Primarily, it is a fun organization full of antics…"with a glorious spirit born when early Clampers lightened the cares of the Gold Rush Days and made the old frontiers ring with laughter."

The Shenandoah Valley

Highway 16 from Sacramento leads along 42 miles of scenic riverbottom ranches and junctions with Highway 49 in Pokerville. The gateway to Shenandoah Valley opens into an expansive seven-square-mile valley tour with over 40 wineries. Branching from the Golden Chain at State Highway 49, leading over a winding roadway through 'Old Pokerville' connecting the Central and Southern Mines, there are several sightseeing trips through Amador's picturesque early redwood, brick, and stone buildings in the area, with beauty matched by its agricultural productivity and the delectable choices of great food

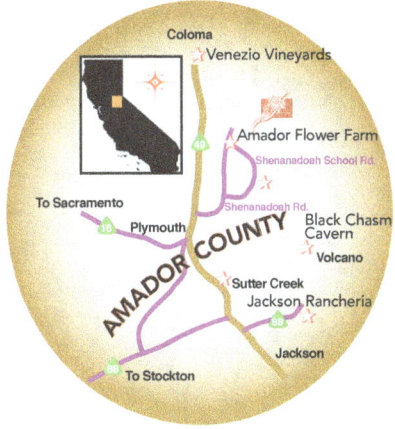

and wine. Shenandoah Valley is perhaps the premier grape-growing region known as the Amador Appellation and a significant producer of historic Old Vine Zinfandel as well, as many other classic California wines.

The Sobon Estate

A Gold Country estate, established in 1977 by the Sobon family with a vineyard appellation growing the best grapes in the Foothills. The Sobon family

pioneered planting Rhône varietals, dessert wines, and harvests from Old Zinfandel grapevines inherited from vines during the Gold Rush. All grapes are 100% estate organically grown, produced and bottled on the premises. These medal-winning wines are recognized nationwide.

D'Agostini Winery

Founded in 1856 by a Swiss immigrant, Adam Uhlinger, with grape vines brought from Europe to Amador County established California's oldest winery with a Registered Historic Landmark museum located at the Sobon Estate Vineyard, built of quarried rock from the nearby Foothills and from hand-hewn beams with original oak casks on display. In 1911, Enrich D'Agostini purchased the winery on 125 acres of vineyards and dedicated his practice to cultivating terroir of the finest wines in loamy soils with California character. He preserved the vineyard's name with the original building and wine cellar. Later, due to decreasing numbers of local purchases and the prohibition of the 1920s, the winery produced wine for sacramental use of the grapes to home winemakers as prescribed under the law. An ideal winemaking climate, the Shenandoah Valley represents an important regional appellation in a vibrant foothill area producing wine.

SIERRA FOOTHILLS UNDERGROUND CAVERN TOURS

1. Black Chasm, Volcano.

2. California Cavern, Cave City.

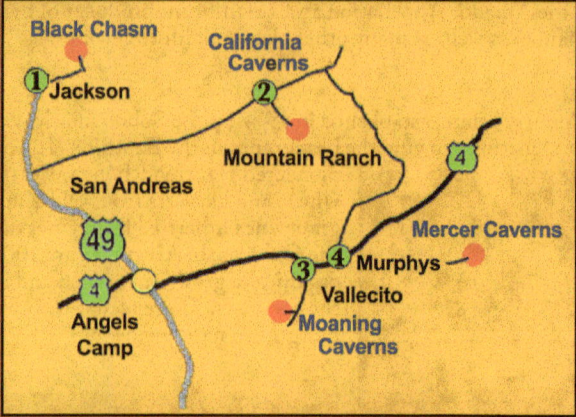

3. Moaning Cavern Hwy 4, in Vallecito.

4. Mercer Caverns, in Murphys.

TOUR 11
CALAVERAS COUNTY
THE GOLDEN PATH OF HISTORY

Hotel Léger was first the Hotel d'France, and established in Mokelumne Hill in 1851.

Beginning in the Calaveras County seat of San Andreas and follow Highway 49 on the Golden Chain trail to a region of the Mother Lode where the notorious robber of stagecoaches, Black Bart met his fate. After his apprehension he was held at the San Andreas Jail and confessed, tried and found guilty there. An even more notorious Gold Country bandit, Joaquin Murrieta was immortalized with the rumors of misdeeds, ravage, and a reign of terror in the open foothills while living in the Mother Lode territory foothills. Along the Highway 49 trail, east of the Mokelumne River at Calaveritas and Mountain Ranch, the fork westward leads to a mining town named in honor of Jenny Lind, the famed opera star known as 'The Swedish Nightingale'. A 49er stop south at Angels Camp brings travelers to an authentic Gold Rush location of the 'Calaveras County Celebrated Jumping Frog Jubilee' written by Mark Twain. The legendary Jumping Frog Jubilee is revived every third week in May and exciting for all attending. A short distance from State Highway 4 at the Highway 49 junction due east, several stopovers of Gold Rush settlements and mining towns include Avery, Vallecito, Murphys and Arnold. On Highway 4, leading towards the Calaveras Big Trees Redwood Sequoias Park, lies within 10 square miles of hiking trails and provides public campsites covered with more than a thousand Giant Redwoods. Some trees 1,000 years or older are up to 25 feet in diameter. Along Highway 4, winter resort accommodations include the Bear Valley Ski Resort and Bear Valley Lodge surrounded by snowy Sierra wonderlands and changing seasonal conditions. From Highway 4 at Ebbett's Pass, travelers connect on journeys towards Lake Tahoe and the Sacramento Gold Country.

The historical Murphys Hotel downtown lodging was visited by US Presidents and other notable travelers. An authentic centerpiece in the Sierra Foothills featuring a period Gold Rush saloon and full-service restaurant.

SAN ANDREAS

In 1848, Mexican settlers named the mining town San Andreas for St. Andrew. The feared bandito, Joaquin Murrieta operated in the 1850's here, and Charles Bolton, known as "Black Bart", wrote poems to his victims. He was convicted of stage robberies and sentenced in the Courthouse. Today, there is a museum and display of his jail cell. Gooney's Saloon, built in 1858 remains at 6 N. Main. The Calaveras County Museum and Archives located at 30 No. Main St. is open 10-4 PM daily, except on major holidays. The Pioneer Cemetery, off Highway 12 is two miles west of San Andreas, and the headstones there describe the dangers often suffered by the early miners. The Courthouse of Calaveras County dates from 1852-1866, and the Hotel Léger, an original hostelry from 1851, first the Hotel d'France, stands prominently on Main Street.

MOKELUMNE HILL

Within a historical district from Main and Center Streets, Old Moke' Hill is a premiere mining town of the Central Gold Country Foothills. A group of Oregon prospectors began mining the river below the town and finding more than enough deposits at the risk of leaving to resupply until starvation set in. One member traveled out, and upon his return set up a tent selling daily provisions earning as much as the miners. The name Mokelumne derived from a Miwuk Indian word possibly translates to 'people of the village of Mukul'. There are ruins of a Chinatown settlement with landmarks and the Hotel Léger dating to 1851, and a few remaining Gold Rush buildings after fires consumed the town. Walking tours to the IOOF Hall built after the fires in 1854, is the first two-story stone building, and later a third story was added in 1861.

Angels Camp's downtown on State Highway 49.

ANGELS CAMP

Founded in June 1848 by Henry and George Angel, Angels Camp was among the earliest of Mother Lode Southern Mining gold camps located between Carson Hill and Altaville, along State Highway 49. The two brothers were first in attempting placer mining along Dead Horse Ravine, Dry Creek, and China Gulch, and chose to settle there naming the streams of Angels Creek. Despite early accounts of placer mining in the area, in a few years, gold discoveries shifted to underground quartz mining. During the mid-1800s, a discovery by the Winter brothers found a large gold vein on Main Street following a long drift of the 49er Mother Lode to the southern edge of town in nearby Altaville. This event mushroomed into five major mines, and the Utica, the Stickle, the Lightner, the Angels, and Sultana mines were developed simultaneously in Angels Camp. Peaking during the 1880s and 1890s, over two hundred stamps were busily pummeling quartz ore throughout the day and night.

In 1857, eight water-driven mills of 70 stamps and four steam mills with 48 stamps were operating in Angels, and by 1885, the chief mine was the Utica from the 1850s. In 1893, the mine produced more than $4,000,000 worth of gold. The total production of the region is estimated at $30,000,000. Henry Angel, the mining camp co-founder, being realistic about the hard work of labor gold mining, became determined to open the Angels Trading Post. His brother, George joining him began selling merchandise inside a simple canvas tent camp, at the intersection of Dry Creek and Angels Creek. In its heyday, a simple pickaxe rung up a $200 sale to its provider, and new cotton shirts might cost $50. Fresh daily provisions came to the early mining camps from supply lines connected to the San Francisco harbor. Within weeks of settlement, 100s of tents were scattered throughout the mile-long placer mines near Angels Trading Post were visible. The name shortened to Angels Camp in 1849, and the population soared to 2,000 miners occupying the gold diggin' streams. The Angel brothers sold the trading post and the buyer, Charles Scribner, became the town postmaster and a Wells Fargo agent. He constructed a massive wooden building at the trading post site later destroyed by fire in 1855, then rebuilt it. The fire consumed tents and outbuildings, and again, new buildings of stone, brick, and iron shutters constructed remain the buildings in view today. The boardwalks lining the edges of the streets lead to several vintage wooden buildings within downtown, many partially recovered from the early fires. Angels Camp is the home to the Jumping Frog Jubilee of Calaveras County, where Mark Twain's frog story leaped to worldwide fame, and is the place where Bret Harte wrote "The Luck of Roaring Camp".

Vallecito

The Murphy brothers, in 1849, found gold in Vallecito. Developing the rich diggings on Coyote Gulch, 'Coyoteing' referred to shaft-size holes dug during dry weather, or from streams with placer finds on wet days. A newspaper described a party of eight men unearthing a lump of 26 pounds, with 25 pounds of pure gold. Soon stories of 10 lb. nuggets were reported in holes dug fifty feet deep. Between 1852 and 1855, shipments of gold valued at $60,000 lasted over a monthly basis into 1867, soon afterwards earning $20,000 each month. The town is situated along an 'ancient river channel' with a concentration of gold ore and is also known for the Moaning Caverns.

The post office was formed in 1854 as Vallecita, "Little Valley", as named by Mexican miners, then changed to today's name in 1940. The historic Vallecito Bell Monument is at Church Street & Cemetery Lane, at the center of town. The famous Moaning Cavern, at the

Moaning Caverns spiral staircase.

GOLD MINING IN CALIFORNIA.
(Library of Congress)

edge of town, offers an underground world of exploration with cave tours, rappelling, gem panning, and zip line adventures for unique adventures. There are three types of traditional walking tours to take visitors 165 feet down into the largest public underground room in California. For those who feel a bit more adventuresome, Moaning Cavern offers rappelling the 165-foot descent, surrounded by spectacular cavern walls. Professional guides teach safety methods, sending you down on an enjoyable expedition. An even more extreme tour includes rappelling and spelunking throughout the deeper passages and canyons, only recommended for 12 and over. The Caverns also offer a gift shop, picnic area, gem mining, and nature trails.

Copperopolis

Located from Angels Camp, 12 miles west on Highway 4, Copperopolis was explored by prospectors and known for 'iron rust' rocks, a landmark they traveled through to the Nevada Comstock Silver mines, in 1860. Finding assays rich in copper valued at $120 per ton, the area was called first Copper Canyon, later changing to Copperopolis during the boom years of large productions of copper ore. Prosperous during the Civil War with shipments arriving to San Francisco, then shipped around Cape Horn and furnished to the Union Army. At the end of the war copper prices dropped over 60%. In 1867, the town engulfed by fire, lost most of its buildings. By the 1870s, the town's population dwindled from thousands to a mere 170. The amount of copper removed added up to over 72,000,000 pounds. Historically, it's at the location where Black Bart's final hold-up caught him in the act of robbing a stage, in 1887. Today, a developed foothill resort and world-class golf resort community, Copperopolis is near the recreational getaway at Lake Tulloch nearby.

Kautz Ironstone Winery was built seven-stories into the ground and features a wine tasting bar with displays of antiques, and an adjoining 1000-acre vineyard. The museum displays an locally mined authentic 80-lb. gold nugget.

The unique Gold Rush fraternal drinking order, E Clampus Vitus, represents years of charitable contributions in the foothills, and documentating history including the impressive outdoor 'Wall of Comparative Ovations', in Murphys.

John Murphy, the town founder.

Murphys

Two brothers, Dan and John Murphy, found gold here in 1849. Murphys Historic Hotel, built by James Sperry and John Perry, was completed in 1856 and opened for business at 457 Main Street. They owned the properties of the Calaveras Big Trees Grove for many years, and the hotel served as a popular tourist destination. Notable guests included Ulysses S. Grant, Mark Twain, and Black Bart, who stayed and dined in the Murphys Hotel. The hotel burned in the fire of 1859, and the stone walls remained and were reused, and rebuilt. The hotel was sold to Frank Mitchler, then operated as the Mitchler Hotel and became a stage depot, bringing visitors to the Big Trees, Bear Valley, and Yosemite.

The landmark Calimbretti / Chase / Mercer House at 350 Main Street built in 1860, was a home to the first American Nobel Prize winner, Albert Michelson. Across from the hotel, the Old Timers Museum on Main Street was built in 1856, as the Peter L. Traver Building and features the outdoor labyrinth-like 'Wall of Comparative Ovations', installed by E. Clampus Vitus as a landmark memorial to the Gold Rush days. The Black Bart Theatre found on Algiers St. is a community playhouse, and Mercer Caverns and Stevenot Winery are found on Sheepranch Rd., each approximately one mile from downtown. The boom in the Murphys mining industries centered at the Oro y Plata Mill was the largest area gold mine and furnished a payroll to the many miners in town. The last operations came from the great 'Glory Hole' found well above the mill, on the ridge near town. Blasting out a giant crater, ore carts were used for taking away aggregate ore for reduction at the stamp mill. The Central Hill Mine located one mile south of Murphys, on the prehistoric Calaveras River, was a profitable deposit of gold in Murphys Flat. At first, the lode ore was tunneled out, but miners converted to 'hydraulicking', powered from high-pressured streams 15 miles away in Murphys Creek Canyon traveling along a flume suspended 190-feet, suspended between two wooden pillars.

Avery

Located on State Highway 4, Avery was the first Euro-American settlement in the region and a well-regarded road stop at first a four-room house and hotel, and a family home. The Avery Historic Hotel, built in 1853, is located between Murphys, Arnold, and Calaveras Big Trees State Park, and is known as the 'Half Way House'. The original boarding house and home were incorporated into the larger hotel. During the 1859 Silver Rush into Nevada's Comstock mines, the hotel became a busy station greeting overland travelers. George Avery purchased the hotel from the original owners in 1869, after 1874 and through the 1900s, operated a store, post office, and his own logging business.

Arnold

A resort community along State Highway 4 offering fine art galleries, restaurants, hiking, camping, winter snowshoeing, cross-country skiing, fishing, swimming, and local breweries. The town lies between Calaveras Big Trees State Park and the mining town of downtown Murphys. The Meadowmont Golf Course, with spectacular resort lodging available just off Highway 4, offers a picturesque golf resort in the high country between Murphys, Bear Valley, and Ebbetts Pass.

Mountain Ranch, Cave City, Sheep Ranch

California Caverns, a landmark located at Cave City, lies 10 miles east of San Andreas off Mountain Ranch Road. It has been open since 1850 with miles of winding underground passages.

Dorrington

Continue east on Highway 4 to the small town of Dorrington. In a setting of lush forests and an inviting place to stop, the historical building, the Dorrington Hotel on Highway 4, was established in 1860 as an original coach stop, hotel, and restaurant.

The 1860s Dorrington Hotel.

Paloma

Mining for Placer gold and underground quartz gold in 1849, William Gwin, California's first U.S. Senator, acquired Paloma in 1851. The Gwin Mine produced millions before closing in 1908.

Douglas Flat

The location of the Central Hill Channel ancient river deposits for vast quantities of gold came with the discovery of gold along Coyote Creek from miners in 1850 reports of 2 lbs a day, the town mushroomed as a roaring tent camp, in 1856. One company had averaged 30 to 50 ounces a day. The Douglas Flat School, the oldest building in Calaveras County, was built in the mid-1850s.

Calaveras Historical Spots

Lancha Plana – Camanche Lake

A California Landmark, the Camanche Lake, once Limerick, lies between the California counties of Amador, Calaveras, and San Joaquin, then renamed for an Iowa town in 1849. Other rich mines named Cat Camp and Sand Hill helped the growing area's population rise to 1,500 during the Gold Rush. Water brought in from Lancha Plana later was inundated as a water resource in 1950, making Camanche Lake. Rich returns from the hill and bluff mining was outstriped river panning for gold. Also, along the Mokelumne River, the Poverty Bar ditch yielded rich rewards and became the mooring place for the flatboat

Carson Hill

After the discovery of the Morgan Mine in 1850 at the summit of Carson Hill, the entire radius around the hill had filled with thousands of miners staking claims within a few miles. Considered the richest gold mining region of California, it is called 'the classic mining ground in California' producing the largest nugget ever taken from the ground, a record at 195 lbs., a discovery made November, 1854. Valued at $43,534 at the time, it was considered the largest in the United States with the mine's total production bearing over $26,000,000. Between Carson Hill and Albany Flat, a little known camp in the forest is where an insurrection between the Americans and Mexicans broke out called the Battle of Six Mile Creek. It was on a road to the creek, Los Muertos, where Chilean and Mexicans miners had grouped was also rumored a favorite of the notorious bandito, Joaquin Murieta.

Several historic sites found on State Highway 49 in Calaveras County include the Altaville Grammar School built in 1859, and Carson Hill where the largest gold nugget was extracted in the western hemisphere weighing in at 195 lbs. The Angels Camp Museum exhibits steam tractor engines, blacksmith and foundry, a working model of stamp mill, mining equipment, a huge overshot Water Wheel, and a large carriage house with 25 carriages and carts. Also, a rock hounds delight! 753 S. Main St. Highway 49, 209-736-2963. 10–4PM daily.

An 1858 provisions store and converted residence in Murphys, on Main Street.

Gold Rush Contemporary
Mark Twain in the Gold Country

Mark Twain in 1867, a photo by Abdullah Frères.

Traveling west with his brother, Orion, by stagecoach from St. Joseph, Missouri into the Nevada Territory, Samuel Langehorne Clemens literally grew up in the Sierra Foothills, leaving behind his boyhood name for the auspicious pen name, Mark Twain. Orion Clemens was appointed by President Lincoln to Secretary of the Nevada Territory in 1861. A move there allowed Mark Twain's first apprenticeship as a writer and reporter, joining the Territorial Enterprise under his mentor, Daniel DeQuille. An American author, journalist and humorist, William Wright, under the name DeQuille, was a respected newspaper writer in Virginia City, Nevada, in 1862. He hired Clemens the following year for $25 a week. It's when Mark Twain choose his adopted pen name. Later, in 1876, Twain wrote the introduction to DeQuille's popular book, the 'Big Bonanza',

citing the tales of the Virginia City 'Silver Rush' beginning 1859, just ten years after the California Gold Rush. Many mining towns experienced a renaissance reemerging from the gold mining period, as the boom in silver had drawn miners to the Nevada Comstock Lode. While in California, Mark Twain invested with partners in a 'pocket' mine and lived the laborious life as described in his book, 'Roughing It'. During his first trip to San Francisco in May, 1863, he made important connections, and by September his works were published in a local literary journal back east. With his newly found acclaim rising from societal literary influences, he was prompted to submit stories to the New York Mercury in 1865, and one that included 'The Celebrated Jumping Frog of Calaveras County', a story that probably originated from a barkeep in

Mark Twain monument in Utica Park, Angels Camp.

Angels Camp. In a famous quote he predicted, "Twenty years from now, you will be more disappointed by the things that you didn't do than by the ones you did do. So throw off the bowlines. Sail away from the safe harbor. Catch the trade winds in your sails. Explore. Dream. Discover."

Gold Rush Street Fairs occurring throughout the Foothills.

SPRINGFIELD

Adjacent to Columbia, the small town of Springfield was known for the appearance of its tidy town square with a first church erected before the first saloon. At the head of Mormon Creek, enough water there allowed 100 men to work the rich placer streams. Known for its sobriety and orderliness of its citizens, many worked at the nearby mines in the Table Mountain area.

DOUBLE SPRINGS

Between Carson Hill and Valley Springs, the town of Double Springs once vied as the Calaveras County seat, before the original lines of Amador County were carved out from its once massive territory. A simple prank of young men distracted the county clerk at a local saloon, after securing the records they brought the county archive to Jackson, then preceded ratifying Jackson as County seat.

VALLEY SPRINGS

Valley Springs changed its name after first choosing Spring Valley, but the name had been used for a town in Colusa County. Grinding rocks and large Valley Oaks were found in Valley Springs, offering clues to the once nomadic Miwuk Indians. By 1849, the first saloon was built in town profiting from the cross-traffic of miners migrating to the Central Gold Country during the Gold Rush. The town is a hub to the Sacramento River Delta, Stockton and Sacramento to the North.

NEW MELONES LAKE

Melones was a rich and expansive mining area between 1895-1918, allied with Carson Hill's Morgan Mine. There was a 100-stamp mill producing ore from all the mines together until it burned down in 1942. Two-miles south of Carson Hill in 1982, New Melones Lake was impounded within the Stanislaus River canyon, with a 100-mile shoreline surrounding the reservoir. Marina rental houseboats, and fishing with a home to eagles, heron, cormorant, grebe, and hundreds of species of wildlife.

A 1000-acre vineyard, Kautz Ironstone Winery in Murphys is just one mile from downtown.

An 80lb. nugget on display at the Kautz Ironstone Winery Heritage Museum is open to the public.

Mark Twain's Golden Adventures

On Mark Twain's returning to California in 1866 from the Sandwich Islands, he began holding audiences as a lecturer holding his famous tours along Highway 49 between Lake Tahoe, Nevada City to Angels Camp, from 1865-66. Regarding the Gold Rush, he stated with quick witted humor, "Few of us can stand prosperity. Another man's, I mean." When he was sojourning in Angels Camp, an original story said to have been described by a saloon keeper, Ben Coon, at the local Tryon's Hotel, sparked Twain's story about a prize jumping frog. The publication back east of his "The Celebrated Jumping Frog of Calaveras County" in 1865 catapulted with his recognition throughout the world of literature.

During the golden days of exploration and traveling to the mining towns, Twain lived as a guest of the Gillis brothers where he camped in the cabin, near Columbia and Jamestown. Named for the burros used by mining pack trains resting on the hill overnight, the cabin was located on Jackass Hill with as many as 200 animals during the boom days along the 49er trails that were known to perform in the evening, filling up the woodlands with their bellowing. At the time when the diggings were still rich in coarse gold, a lucky miner working a few hours a day could still build a fortune. Some claims at 100-square feet yielded as much as $10,000. Despite his boredom of writing columns as a correspondent for Nevada's Virginia City Territorial Enterprise, he had sent daily letters of his exploits and encounters to be carried in several

Central Gold Country

daily papers. The letters Twain sent to the Sacramento Union newspaper after visiting the Sandwich Islands were the basis of his traveling lectures. A featured highlight became the serious dramatic descriptions of Kilauea's fiery volcano, with other travel stories that delighted the audience. During one incident, Twain would never forget a logging scheme devised with a partner ending in a sudden disaster along the forested edge of Lake Tahoe at the Nevada line. His plans were devoured after lighting a simple campfire and setting off a conflagration destroying the entire forest as the entire project, camp and timber harvest burnt up. A winding road perched over Crystal Bay is the historical fire lookout and small park where Twain climbed to view the water's edge and territory below - on a hilltop high above the mountain waters looking due south over the 'Lake Of The Sky'.

From the beginning, Twain's lectures included antics with ideas for cleverly advertised appearances. In Nevada County, the Grass Valley Daily Union ad with his Nevada County appearance, Twain promised that after the lecture he would perform a series of "wonderful feats of SLEIGHT OF HAND, if desired to do so." It's said one of his feats involved drinking multiple shots of whiskey, then leaving town suddenly without paying his hotel bill. Frequently, his advertisements would state "the doors will open at 7 o'clock, and the trouble will begin at 8."

During one lecture, he agreed to link his appearance with a tightrope act appearing in town with the circus act of Rosa Celeste, who a few days earlier in Rough and Ready had gone further than expected after a harmless accident. During her act, it appeared that she was about to fall. And, a miner in the audience rushed forward to catch her in a wheelbarrow that ended up landing on the miner's head. With his head poked through the bottom of the wheelbarrow, he ended up with the bottomless wheelbarrow draped over his shoulders. A journal in 1880 recounted, "The man suffered no injury ...but what a few drinks of whiskey could repair." Twain wisely declined to be double-billed with street carnival attractions after this. He personally recounted his subjects in a comical style describing their characteristics, habits, vices and virtues. During the conclusion, theaters rang with a thunderous applause.

On curtain calls, he jokingly apologized to the audience for "inflicting his lecture upon them, and that he needed the money." Mark Twain's performances were embellished frequently by clever maxims and memorable quotes such as, "It's better to keep your mouth shut and appear stupid than to open it removing all doubt," as well as, "You can't depend on your eyes when your imagination is out of focus." His personal philosophy, "Always do right. This will gratify some people and astonish the rest." As a professional entertainer, one critic summed up in the San Francisco Evening Bulletin, "He displayed not the polish of the finished lecturer—nor did he need it; the crude, quaint delivery was infinitely preferable." Another remarking on Twain's performance, "his method as a lecturer was distinctly unique and novel. Speaking with a slow, deliberate drawl, and anxious and perturbed expectation in his visage, adding an apparent painful show of effort as he framed his sentences ....all original, Mark Twain's folksy, comical style always was presented in a serious demeanor."

Black Bart – Touch of a Po8

Charles E. Boles was a stoic and a rather elite personality who transformed himself into a stealthy bank robber with an underlying passion in holding up Wells Fargo stagecoaches and removing personal articles from the passengers along with the contents of the company's strongbox. After his first heist in Sonoma County's Russian River area in 1877, he halted a Wells Fargo stagecoach with a double-barreled shotgun pointed at the driver. When the dust settled, a search by the posse found only a small paper with a poem written by the robber stating, "I've labored long and hard for bread, for honor, and for riches, but on my corns too long you've tread, you fine-haired sons of bitches", signed 'The Po8'. Black Bart's calling card soon became well known from his respectful good manners while robbing his victims, and dominated headlines of the local San Francisco papers calling attention to his Wells Fargo stickups for large sums of gold and valuables. Black Bart struck again in July 1878, near the Feather River between Quincy and Oroville, stepping out of the bushes at a difficult turn in the trail, armed and again demanding the strong box thrown down. That day he lifted $379, a silver watch, diamond ring, and left a carefully composed round of verse with a message boasting, "if there's money in that box 'tis munny in my purse!" Wells Fargo and the Governor started investigations and offered a reward totaling $600, plus an additional $200 from Postal authorities. Black Bart remained on the lam another five years and continued carrying out several notorious robberies. All the while living incognito in San Francisco, he reportedly covered himself by walking on foot to each heist, avoiding any tell-tale horse or foot tracks. The end came in 1883 while testing Black Bart's stealth and prowess, holding up another stagecoach on the way towards Copperopolis in the Gold Country. The strongbox bolted to the floor held $550 in gold coin, over three ounces of gold dust, and 228 ounces of a gold amalgam from the nearby Patterson Mine. Black Bart seemingly was aware of the amalgam while ordering the stage driver down and making him unhitch the team to walk them up the hill. The 'Po8' robber proceeded clearing out the chest's contents, but while backing out of the carriage was fired upon by the stage driver, then fired at by a passenger just returning to the stage after hunting in the backwoods with his Henry rifle. Although the driver missed twice, the passenger made his mark and Black Bart was seen slightly staggered making his escape. The investigation located evidence, including a small round derby hat, two bags containing flour, crackers, and sugar, a leather case with field glasses, a belt, quartz magnifying glass, razor, and one handkerchief full of buckshot. A soiled laundry tag proved to be the clue Wells Fargo needed tracking down its owner, and within a week identified Boles as Charles E. Bolton, or the notorious Black Bart. Facing his fate at trial in the San Andreas courtroom of Calaveras County, he gave back the stolen amalgam and confessed to his dark deeds. After 28 stage robberies, Black Bart received a six-year sentence at San Quentin Prison, shortened to four years for good behavior. As the story goes after his release, the highwayman vanished into the dustbin of history, never to be seen or heard from again.

Black Bart, in 1888.

CALAVERAS BIG TREES STATE PARK

On Highway 4, four-miles east of Arnold at a 4,500 foot elevation, the 'Mammoth Trees' of Calaveras Big Trees State Park compise two stands of Giant Sequoias totaling more than 1,000 trees rising up to 325' in height with trunks twice the size their cousins, the Coastal Redwoods. Visitors take in eight miles of hiking trails through spectacular groves in their natural setting. Calaveras Big Trees State Park features 6,498 acres of Sequoia Redwoods and lava outcroppings at the scenic canyon on the North Fork of Stanislaus River with 129 campsites, guided hikes, campfire talks and camp sites, picnicking, fishing, swimming, and nature trails.
For reservations, 800-444-PARK.

CALAVERAS LODGING AND VISITOR ASSOCIATION
753 S. MAIN ST., ANGELS CAMP 95222   209-736-0049

The New Melones Bridge follows Highway 49's southern trail to Jamestown, Columbia State Historic Park, Sonora and Mariposa.

Gold Rush State Historic Parks

Columbia State Historic Park
11255 Jackson St, Columbia, CA 95310 209-588-9128

Considered 'The Gem of the Southern Mines' on State Highway 49, Columbia State Historical Park in the Central Mother Lode Mining District is accessed from Shaws Flat Road or Springfield Road. During the early Gold Rush, the Columbia region first was the placer mines at Hildreth Diggins, American Camp, and Dry Diggins, and known for incredible gold discoveries. Dr. Thaddeus Hildreth and his brother, George, noticed flakes of gold stuck to their wet blanketing and word spread immediately into surrounding camps, and over 6,000 curious miners relocated there within the next month. During its heyday, 20,000 people converged at one spontaneous tent camp and soon established four banks, eight hotels, 27 stores, 30 saloons, a school, two churches, and hosted 143 Faro games in Columbia. The surrounding 300 acres produced millions of dollars of gold and left behind a landscape of pale ghostly limestone rocks eerily projecting above the surface. Early newspaper reports from 1850-1852 cited several large and one nearly pure gold nugget

Visitors at Columbia State Historic Park's sluice box for panning gold.

found by an itinerant valued by Wells Fargo at $14,000, weighing 72 lbs. Another, at 33.5 lbs., was purchased for $7,438.50. After 1860, estimates were valued at $85,000,000 to $150,000,000 in gold that was dug, picked, or sluiced at Columbia State Historic Park. The news of the gold discovery in 1848 at the dawn of the California Gold Rush brought consistent streams of migrants and spontaneous small tent camps springing up within Tuolumne County, with the towns of Sonora, Columbia, Jamestown, Angels, and Twain Harte, as busy centers of activity and commerce. The region provides countless recreational diversions, including skiing, watersports, houseboating, caving, kayaking and river rafting.

IV. Southern Gold Country

Tour 12
Tuoloume County

Stage Coach rides from the Columbia Wells Fargo, gold panning, restaurants, and blacksmith shops are all part of Columbia State Historic Park activities.

Columbia

Of the lineage of successful mining towns along the State Highway 49 Golden Chain during the 1849 Gold Rush, Columbia State Historic Park is perhaps the finest example of a well-preserved Old West gold town in California. The town's buildings were subjected to devastating fires swept through in 1854 and 1857, and virtually overnight the town rebuilt brick structures successively on a more elaborate scale adding new hotels, saloons, boarding houses, restaurants, laundries, express offices, and tent stores. The town also presented enterprising Argonauts a much easier way to acquire gold by mining the pockets of miners. The old town of Columbia's red brick brightens the scene and visitors are encouraged to hop aboard the Wells Fargo Stage Coach, try panning for gold, meander the streets within walking distance to step into the Saloon and order a Sarsaparilla, then browse many authentically recreated mercantile shops, theaters, hotels, and even a blacksmithing shop. The scarcity of women there gave rise to the popularity of theaters showcasing famous entertainers such as Lotta Crabtree and Lola Montez, as appreciative audiences flung gold coins and nuggets on stage during evening performances in a tinkling delighting the onlookers. The traditions of the California Gold Rush in Columbia provides unlimited varieties of recreational destinations, good fun, and colorful historical events.

Founded in 1848, Sonora, an exquisite Gold Country town was settled by gold miners from Sonora Mexico before the population increased to 5,000, by 1850.

Sonora

At first, Sonorian Camp began as a colorful placer mining town and is the Tuolumne County seat of Sonora today. The town invites visitors to the legendary highlights of a charming 49er western Victorian town from the gold mining days, given the moniker 'Queen of the Southern Mines'. Many downtown destinations are sophisticated brick

'The Red Church' or St. James Episcopal Church from 1860.

and adobe structures occupied currently as historical lodging, shops, and restaurants with several authentic museums, including an iconic County Courthouse. Originally, Sonora was settled in 1848, and early Gold Rush structures appeared during the 1850s with the Gunn House on Washington Street, the 1853 IOOF Hall at North Washington and the oldest Episcopal building in California, the stately red church St. James Episcopal Church from 1859 on the hill above the town. The Tuolumne County Museum and History Center was built in 1857 at 158 W. Bradford St., and opens from 10AM-4PM Mon-Sat. A large adobe-style hotel built in 1896, The Sonora Inn catered to many famous guests from the Golden Era of Hollywood. The Sonora Opera

Sonora's Firehouse Museum and Senior Lounge downtown on Washington St.

House, The Sierra Repertory Theatre, East Sonora Theatre, 13891 Mono Way, Sonora, and Fallon House Theatre at 11175 Washington St. in Columbia, are mainstay community theaters presenting live performances over the decades. At the top of Piety Hill near Sonora High School, the sports field there is probably the best example of a 'pocket' mine and its unusual history at the Bonanza Mine. First located by Chileans carrying valuable surface placers away, the mine was purchased in the 1870s by three prospectors for next to nothing working persistently for years, until one day the miners broke through to a continuous solid vein where one shipment to the San Francisco Mint earned $160,000. The mine started making $500,000 on average weeks until its eventual decline and final sale. Nearby, San Giuseppe and Golden Gate Mines added to estimated totals in the area making around $40,000,000 within a two-mile radius. Contact the Tuolumne Visitors Bureau at 800-446-1333.

Walking tours in town reveal the two-story Sugg House from 1855, with several massive stone and brick buildings nearby.

JAMESTOWN

Downtown Jamestown, Main Street.

A prominent Tuolumne County Gold Rush mining town on Highway 49, Jamestown is the location of legendary placer gold discoveries. Its first goldfield named for the founder, George F. James in August 1848, gave the town its nickname 'Jimtown' and adored by generations in search of an authentic Gold Country mining experience. The collection of original Old West buildings in downtown stretches across the raised boardwalks and porticoes with historical lodging at the Jamestown Hotel and the National Hotel and dining all day, each with authentic 49er saloons and outdoor patios.

At the Rev. James Woods' placer mine at Woods Crossing, one of the most lucrative panning locations of surface mining was discovered to be somewhat remarkable. After taking placers out of the creek ranging from $200-$300 a day per man, earnings increased to more gold than any other creek. Woods Creek was equally as prolific along its two branches of Sullivan's and Curtis Creeks. Montezuma, a busy stopover serving two-stage lines for mining operations in the Summer and Fall of 1852 was stationed on Highway 49, three miles south of Jamestown. The town grew with several legendary deep extensive mines producing exceptionally pure gold. Quartz Mountain, south of Jamestown and east of Highway 49 is a famous producing mine from 1909, added $6,500,000 in gold bullion, then shut down from a decimating fire in 1927. Stent, formerly named Poverty Hill, stands at the location of the old cemetery grounds. Often woven into Bret Harte's

Table Mountain is a nearly 3.7-mile level trail loop on a level 600-feet above ground, along an ancient riverbed.

Wood's Creek is a center of placer gold discoveries from the earliest Gold Rush days and known for lucrative finds and large gold strikes even in recent years.

tales, the prominent geographical landmark of Table Mountain rises visibly over Shaws Flat Road linking backroads into Columbia, Tuttletown, and Jamestown. Dominating the valley with a prominent view from the road, Table Mountain was once an ancient river bed consisting of a large inverted prehistoric mass of lava forming a ledge one-quarter mile wide at a forty-mile length above the valley. It is known for its popular hiking trails, a lake, wildflowers, and moderate terrain.

In 1850, camps along the streams feeding the Tuolumne River created many of the largest settlements in the county. Thousands of miners were engaged in alternate attempts of diverting the water and exposing the ancient riverbeds of aggregate base, full of mineral wealth.

Wood's Creek in 'Old Jimtown' provides a trove of gold panning activities.

CALIFORNIA STATE RAILROAD MUSEUM RAILTOWN 1897

The 1897 Railtown roundhouse and rail turntable.

A Gold Country railroading experience awaits visitors to Jamestown at 5th Ave. & Reservoir Rd. The Railtown 1897 State Historic Park is four miles south of Sonora on Highway 49 and greets visitors with authentic steam trains with unique heritage tours viewing popular Hollywood feature film and television sets dating from the 1920s, and later. The stacks of props from previous movies may be seen in the background within the buildings when attending exciting living history events at the Railtown 1897 Museum. The original offices, station houses and shops from 1897 through 1910 include the unusual central Roundhouse rail turntable on display. From the 200 movies, television programs, and commercials filmed at Railtown, famous titles include The Unforgiven, Back to the Future III, High Noon, The Virginian, Petticoat Junction, and The Wild, Wild, West. A transportation center of mining and timber products, the station primary was the motivation in building the railway. By 1906, the Jamestown complex became a self-contained facility fully capable of repairing or rebuilding locomotives. Catch passage aboard a steam train ride through the foothills and plains on one of the oldest railroads in the West operated by the California State Railroad Museum, in Jamestown. Call for more information: 209-984-3953.

Steam train excursions are available at Jamestown's Railtown 1897 State Park. (Courtesy of the Sacramento Railroad Museum).

TUTTLETOWN

Along the Bret Harte-Mark Twain Trail, Tuttletown is just seven miles from Sonora between Jamestown and Melones, and a booming Gold Rush campsite named for its pioneer founder, Judge Anson A.H. Tuttle. He constructed the first permanent log cabin in Tuolumne County in 1848. Just south of the New Melones Bridge on Highway 49 and across from Jackass Hill, Tuttletown was mined by Mormons and called Mormon Gulch in 1849. The town built a stamp mill in 1851 with reports of five men removing 40 pounds of gold in five days. The Post Office was built in 1857 and Bill Sewer's Stone Store, though no longer standing was frequented by Mark Twain's fondness for swapping stories and rumors of Bret Harte having clerked there.

A single-story Gold Country iron-shuttered store built of chiseled stone and wood, near Shaws Flat Rd. between Jamestown and Table Mountain.

JACKASS HILL

Crossing over the New Melones Bridge into Tuolumne County, a left turn on the Golden Chain Highway 49 South leads to where Mark Twain lived during the winter of 1864-1865, at his cabin on Jackass Hill. Just west of Tuttletown and Columbia State Historic Park. Twain was a guest of the local miners, the Gillis brothers. His friend Steve Gillis frequented a saloon in Angels Camp with him and soon Twain returned to write "Jim Smiley and his Jumping Frog". The story became wildly popular after Bret Harte arranged to publish it in The Californian, under "The Celebrated Jumping Frog of Calaveras County". Twain's masterpiece is revived every third week in May, during Calaveras County's Spring Celebration.

The Mark Twain cabin was the humorist's residence as a guest in the Gold Country.

Moccasin became a thriving gold camp at the mouth of Moccasin Creek, now the site of the Hetch Hetchy water system and powerhouse fed by the Tuolumne River.

MOCCASIN

The City of San Francisco owns the Hetch Hetchy Reservoir serving the residents in the City of San Francisco, 115 miles from Hetch Hetchy Dam. The construction of the controversial dam was signed into law in December 1913 by President Wilson. News of the impending project was vehemently opposed by the naturalist John Muir but eventually inundated with the Hetch Hetchy Valley Dam. Muir held that Hetch Hetchy was a magnificent wild area and a sister to Yosemite Park replicating its magnificence and beauty. Today, the reservoir supplies about 85% of the water supply of the Bay Area.

The Iron Door Saloon is one of the earliest Gold Country establishments standing along State Highway 120 in Groveland, around 30 miles from Yosemite's North Gate.

GROVELAND

A vigilante justice town where spur-of-the-moment trials convicted and condemned murderers and horse thieves by hanging, Groveland was named First Garrote during the earliest Gold Rush days. By 1850, 2,000 Mexican miners had rapidly vanished in fear of the American miners. The Gold Rush town changed its name to Groveland in 1875 and located on State Highway 120, high above the Moccasin Reservoir at Highway 49. The Groveland Hotel, a massive intact adobe built there by George Reed, an area sawmill owner, completed the hotel between 1849 and 1852.

YOSEMITE GATEWAY MUSEUM

State Highway 120 remains the gateway to Yosemite National Park and passes through the Groveland community of 20,000. The Southern Tuolumne County Historical Society recently opened the Gold Country Gateway Museum devoted to the Gold Rush, and the history of Yosemite National Park. The museum advances its goals with preservation projects promoting community education and serving as the local historical resource center at 18990 CA-120, Main St., Groveland. Open Fri-Sun, 10-2PM, 209-962-0300.

The front porch at the Groveland Hotel.

In Chinese Camp, the Rosenblolum Store from 1851 is built of stone and adobe, as with many Gold Rush buildings with an added veneer brick front.

PRIESTS STATION

The old Priest Grade, about a mile from Big Oak Flat follows an original wagon trail up the mountain ridge directly above the Moccasin Creek. Rising to the elevation of 1,575 feet with vistas above the Moccasin Reservoir, an early-stage transported travelers to Yosemite Park required the stage drivers to request passengers walk the grade to relieve the teams barely managing under a load the steep mountain's incline.

CHINESE CAMP

Between the camps Montezuma and Jacksonville, the entry into the Southern Gold Rush mines of Highway 49 enters the crossroads town of colorful downtown Chinese Camp. Highway 49 begins a journey south into Mother Lode towns where Chinese settlers once were imported into California as laborers for the mines, hauling stones and gravel, building the railways and living in the surrounding tent camps and mining towns. Several Englishmen to arrive at the Chinese Camp in 1849 employed Chinese migrants, and founded as Camp Washington a claim just adjacent to an American camp. At the end of 1849 the name became Chinese

Passing an old feed barn off the Highway 120 junction at Highway 49, leading south to Chinese Camp.

Diggins and expanded into a metropolis center of commerce, offering many urban comforts. Renamed Chinese Camp, the town was headquarters for the Yosemite-bound stage lines in the 1850s. Large quantities of placer gold was collected in the region until 1870 after uncovering surface finds from the hills, flats, and streams. Total production rose to around $2,500,000 in gold from the Chinese Camp area, and mining continued there through 1899. The noted author and great American frontiersman, botanist, and biologist, John J. Audubon kept records after visiting the town in 1850. The Chinese Camp Post Office opened in 1854 permanently adopting the name, with an increasing population of over 1,000 in 1856. The main street is still titled Washington and from casual inspection reveals an abandoned ghost-town building or two hidden within the streets of this once-busy Gold Rush crossroads.

The old Post Office in Chinese Camp from 1854 served as a general supply stop for tourists traveling by stagecoach to Yosemite.

La Grange

The town of La Grange was located by pioneering French migrants who jumped ship in San Francisco to commandeer a small boat reaching the gold mines. Named French Camp after the sailors camped on the Stanislaus River, mining abundant riches by panning the shores. The town was named La Grange after opening its Post Office in 1854, and in a few years the settlement grew to thousands and was a crossroads of trade over a wide area and supported three stage lines. Surrounded by the agricultural bottomland perfect of raising grains in the region, the first flour mill was built in the 1850s, but the town eventually lost prominence through multiple disasters from the immense winter rain storms in 1856, flooding the town and destroying the flour mill. Tragedy again struck in 1861, and winter floods washed the mining claims down the river. Many Chinese had returned there to rework the claims after the mines were swept away.

In downtown La Grange, a saloon occupies the bottom floor of the old IOOF building.

The survivors of town rebuilt along the J132, a county road 21 miles west of Coulterville, on State Highway 49. There are prominent mine tailings visible along the riverbanks and several Gold Rush buildings remain.

Knights Ferry

In a tribute to the town founder, Knights Ferry Bridge crosses the Stanislaus River today on a 379-foot long covered wooden bridge built in 1863, and the longest covered bridge west of the Mississippi. Its earliest settler, Knight left his first home along the Sacramento River in Yolo County in 1841, relocating from Knights Landing with his family to stake a claim on the Stanislaus River in 1849. He established a trading post and set up a crossing over the swift river current. His ferry boat was made from an old whaling boat and powered by using the

Knights Ferry Covered Bridge on the Stanislaus River was completed in 1857.

Southern Gold Country

flowing water against its rudder and making crossings navigated by a cable harnessed to guide the boat over the river. Pay tolls supported Knight and his partner, James Vantine. The river crossing became the main route for travelers to Port Stockton for gold bullion shipments arriving in San Francisco. At its peak, the receipts piled up to $500 per day but tragically in November, Knight was struck unexpectedly and maliciously gunned down. The enterprise passed to his partner, Vantine, who sold it and returned east. In 1857, after a new covered bridge was built passage tolls were set at $1 for a horse and oxen team, 75¢ for horse and buggies, 50¢ for horses with riders, 20¢ for livestock, hogs, sheep, or goats for 10¢, and foot traffic 25¢. The winter of 1862 brought driving rains along the river with water rising above the 30-foot level drowning the town, wiping out buildings and destroying the bridge. The rebuilt 1863 wooden Knights Ferry Covered Bridge remains a remarkable piece of craftsmanship reflecting the history of the California Gold Rush.

JACKSONVILLE – LAKE DON PEDRO

Jacksonville was established in June 1849 by Colonel Alden Jackson, a Mexican War veteran and soon became a central trading post in the valley of the Tuolumne River, at the junction of Woods Creek. A pioneer settler, Julian S. Smart began clearing trees and brush planting the first gardens and orchards in the county calling them Spring Garden. The town soon rivaled nearby Sonora in its size by 1851. Mining operations supplanted the property and produced tremendous earnings totaling over $9,000,000 of gold by 1926. In 1923, the construction of Lake Don Pedro Dam inundated Jacksonville and created nearly 120 miles of a shoreline and resort. Visitors driving State Highway 49 today enjoy vacations of fishing, houseboating, boating, rafting, kayaking, swimming, and camping at Gold Country Foothill destinations that include New Melones Lake and nearby Yosemite National Park, each perfect destinations for overnight and extended vacation rentals.

Houseboating along the Stanislaus and Tuolumne Rivers make relaxing vacations and retreats off Highway 49, near Yosemite National Park.

NATIONAL FOREST WILDERNESS AREAS

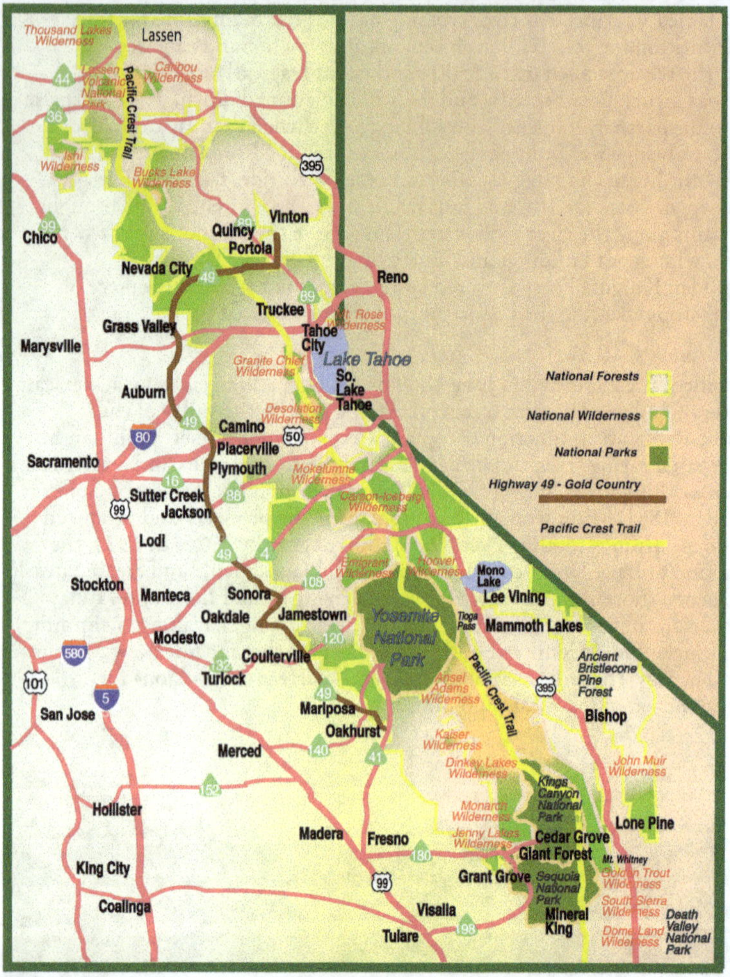

TOUR 13
MARIPOSA COUNTY
THE YOSEMITE GATEWAY

Mariposa County Courthouse from 1850 is a Gold Country landmark. The seat of Mariposa County, the building stands along traditional access outes to Yosemite National Park. along the Golden Chain on State Highway 49.

MARIPOSA COUNTY COURTHOUSE

In Mariposa on Bullion Street between Ninth and Tenth Street, the 1854 Mariposa County Courthouse is the oldest California-style example of Greek Revival architecture, west of the Mississippi River. The the historic courthouse over the years improved by adding more modernized facilities while maintaining its original appearance. Mariposa County, one of the original 27 counties in California drawn from the boundary lines of 1850 and equaling approximately 30,000 square miles over one-fifth of the state's total area. It became a modest 1,455 square miles after the influx of miners from the Gold Rush brought in the highest population during the Gold Rush, through the 1850's.

On July 21, 1854, the contract awarded for $9,000 built the 50ft. x 40ft. two-story wooden building by the end of that year. The logs for the building were felled less than a mile from the site and cut with a sawmill powered by a wood-burning steam engine. A tall stand of white pine beams were held in-place with pine pegs, then strengthened from mortise and tenon joints with no nails used. The wood was finished using hand-planing in a rustic tongue-and-groove style. On close examination, the spectator's benches, counsel tables, jury box, and judge's bench have the carpenter's plane marks exposed, also visible along

Mariposa is known for butterflies and wildflower walks.

the interior walls. The front downstairs hall displays several artifacts unearthed during the 1987-88 restoration project. The courthouse, accepted as a National Historic Landmark has provided some of the most celebrated and noted civil, mining, and water law cases litigated in its courtroom. Cases of ownership rights included the massive Frémont land title, and the Biddle Boggs vs. Merced Mining Company case. During the 1954 Centennial celebrations, the State Bar recognized the significance of the courthouse by declaring it as a "preserved shrine to justice in California."

Upon entering the courthouse and looking to the right side displays of rancher cattle brands and earmarks, visitors step back to the history of the early Alta California era. On the left in the main hall, the portrait exhibits of all of the county's Superior Court Judges line the right side of the wall. And left past the main hall stairway leading to the 1935 addition is where the authentic maps of counties divided from Mariposa County's original borderlines are displayed. The addition of a safekeeping vault holds the county records back to 1861. The most famous changes to the structure include the cupola and clock. From March through July of 1866, the Board of Supervisors was subjected to criticism concerning the clock from the editor of the Mariposa Gazette. The bill of sale at $1,130.35 including freight for the bell made in 1861 has the mark of Taylor Vickers & Co., Sheffield imprinted and weighs 267 lbs. The clock that featured four faces and was shipped around the Horn from the East Coast and must be wound once a week by hand-cranking two weighted cables on separate drums to activate the bell. After the long-running timepiece lasted generations, the newspaper regarding the clock's installation offered the concession, "It is humming away now and is quite an improvement to the place."

Over decades, a two-story Mariposa Courthouse Annex added to the original 1854 building doubled the original length as it appears today. In 1891, a vault cost $1,800 and in 1895, a telephone was installed in the Clerk's office; then by 1900, a four-office annex building was added at a of cost $1,400. In 1907, an upgrade to modern electric lighting in the Clerk's office and last expansion of any consequence began in February 1935, establishing a State Emergency Relief Administration with new restrooms added inside. Visitor info, 209-966-7081.

Highway 49 traverses switchbacks with its ascent above the Merced River on the way to Oakhurst.

CALIFORNIA STATE MINING & MINERAL MUSEUM

Mariposa County Fairgrounds and the California State Mining and Mineral Museum each occupy a stretch of Highway 49 frontage, just south of town. The museum contains a diversity of California's great mineral history and wealth, with over 13,000 objects including mining artifacts, rare specimens of gold, stunning gem and mineral specimens. Moved from an original collection in San Francisco, the museum became a California State Park in 1999. On display, the Fricot 'Nugget' weighing 13.8 lbs., is a rare beautiful specimen of crystallized gold discovered in the American River in 1864. Most similar ones were often melted down. A mining tunnel and working scale model stamp mill helps explain how gold was produced during the Gold Rush.

Gold Rush Contemporary
John C. Frémont 'The Pathfinder'

Republican Candidate 1856 political poster.

America's military defenses were stationed in California by land and at sea after 1823, and subjected to the expansion of brazen Mexican Californio's horse and cattlemen running roughshod over the disbanded old Spanish missionary towns. American fur trappers had made paths into Alta California's territories and the first topographical expedition of 1842 was led by Kit Carson, a trail-blazing scout, with Captain John C. Frémont known as the 'The Pathfinder'. A second expedition in 1845 by Carson and Frémont would endure starvation during a frostbitten winter, as worn American volunteers crossed the Sierra barely surviving the severe storms arriving at Sutter's Fort and welcomed by Captain John Sutter. Sutter graciously outfitted Frémont's company with food, lodging, and fresh horses. Frémont, aware of the increasing interest of Americans living in California published the exploratory maps he made in 1845, an invaluable resource for overland expeditions into Oregon, Utah, and California. In early 1846, a decisive war against Mexico City's reign began on several fronts, and the Americans secured Monterey by sea. Major Frémont was appointed to command the California Battalion leading 428 men to capture Santa Barbara and Los Angeles. The 1847 Treaty of Cahuenga ended those hostilities, with Commodore Stockton rewarding Major Frémont to 'Military Governor'.

Frémont, 'The Pathfinder'. (Library of Congress)

The US Army overseen by Brigadier General Kearny with victory at the Battle of San Pasquale ended the Mexican war with the signing of the 1848 Treaty of Hildago. After refusing Kearny's orders to relinquish his Governorship and legitimacy of Fremont's command led to a court-martial dispute, and the case settled against Frémont for subordination and mutiny charges. The sentence was commuted later by President Polk in 1850 allowing Frémont to be one of two new US Senators from California. In 1856, he became the first candidate to campaign for the US Presidency in the new Republican party and lost to John Buchanan. Frémont also served in the Civil War, and from 1878 to 1881, President Rutherford B. Hayes appointed him governor of the Arizona Territory. He wrote his best-selling book on his travels with the help of his wife, Jesse Frémont, daughter of the famed US Senator Thomas Hart Benton.

The junction of Highway 49 and Mariposa County J132, where the old Hotel Jeffrey stands as the largest intact building in the town.

COULTERVILLE

Taking Highway 120 from Modesto, an alternative way to the northwest gate of Yosemite begins at the junction of Highway 49, in the charming Mariposa County outpost of old Coulterville, on the Golden Chain. At the intersection of County J132, the highway passes Hetch Hetchy Valley Reservoir via State Highway 120 to Buck Meadows, and the Big Oak Flat Gate on the northeast corner. The road proceeds through Yosemite Valley and passes the scenic Tuolumne and Merced Grove of Giant Sequoias. During his explorations in Hetch Hetchy Valley during 1903, John Muir began the environmental protest of alarm directed against the construction at this remote landscape, adjacent to Yosemite. He stated it to be a setting as wild and magnificently as grand. Later, the land was inundated in 1923 to supply fresh water into the Bay Area. Countless efforts to reversing and reopening the Hetch Hetchy Valley continues to promote restoration and its conservation value. John Muir noted the exact mirroring of Hetch Hetchy to its famed next-door neighbor Yosemite.

In 1849, the first settlers coming from Pennsylvania in the area, George and Margaret Coulter, set a supply camp up on the 49er trail. Above their blue canvas tent flew a conspicuous American Flag called by the miners 'Banderita', or 'Little Flag', flying red, white, and blue. In time, Coulterville purported to be "The Gold Rush Town Too Tough to Die!" after the scourge of frequent fires and building losses were endured during 1859, 1879, and 1899, and leveling much of the original settlement. The buildings consumed by fire were beyond repair except for the Sun Sun Wo Co. Store, an adobe of rammed earth constructed by Chinese miners in 1851. At the junction of Highway 49 and J132, the Hotel Jeffrey, the largest remaining intact building, was built after the fire of 1903 on the original building foundations from 1851 using nearly three-foot thick adobe brick walls. Connected to the Jeffrey Hotel, a true landmark the Magnolia Room opens into a large authentic Gold Rush establishment displaying a 40-foot polished bar top. It was one of 25 saloons and 10 hotels during the town's early heyday.

Whistling Billy run by the Merced Mining Company in 1897, is an eight-ton wood burning locomotive in Coulterville's center.

Placer mining brought thousands to the area at several creeks around the area panning placer gold, but soon gold nuggets became scarce. In 1852, hard rock mining turned the town around and new thriving industrial operations brought miners from around the world. The mills expanded with one mine using 20 stamps continuously extracting ore from mined gravel in the diggings. In 1856, Wells Fargo & Co. established a building of brick in the 1870s managed by Nelson Cody, the brother of Buffalo Bill Cody. The town still features iconic historic buildings, including a blacksmith shop, bandstand, jail, powder house, warehouse, general store and museum. The gold mines are mostly gone today except for the names imprinted into the town's history based on $15 to $35 values for gold. In the last part of the 19th Century, the Louisa Mine produced nearly $100,000 with the Mary Harrison Mine, Virginia Mine, Malvina Mine

Welcome to the Jeffrey Hotel's Magnolia Room and smooth 1890s bar top, with an array of notecards and memorabilia traditionally left pinned to the ceiling.

Southern Gold Country 187

The Mariposa Museum and History Center is visible on Highway 49 in Coulterville, with displays of mineral samples and mining equipment from the Gold Rush days.

Group, Marble Springs Mine, Bandarita Mine, and California's first patent mine, the Penon Blanco Mine collectively producing in the millions of dollars.

WHITEWATER RAFTING IN THE SOUTHERN GOLD COUNTRY

The Grand Canyon of the Tuolumne River is an outstanding whitewater adventure near Yosemite National Park featuring Class IV rapids for over 18 miles. Trips for Class III on the main Stanislaus or 'Camp 9' run may be obtained, and the Southern Gold Country Merced River is recommended for first-timers or previous paddlers. Check with local river outfitters providing river rafting trips in the area for scheduled day trips, overnight glamping, and camp-outs with whitewater experiences.

On Highway 49, an old remaining stone edifice reflects on Bear Valley's colorful historical past.

A southwest view in Lee Vining on Tioga Pass from US Highway 395, beginning a steep incline towards Yosemite's eastern gate at Tuolumne Meadows.

YOSEMITE NATIONAL PARK
TOUR 14

Tenaya Lake, near Olmsted Point.

YOSEMITE PARK'S FOUR ENTRY GATES

Northwest Entrance – From State Highway 99 in Modesto or Manteca, take a 90-mile drive east to Yosemite following State Highway 120. At junction in Coulterville and Highway 49, the County Road J132 heads towards Buck Meadows passing Hetch Hetchy Reservoir. Continue on State Highway 120 to Big Oak Flat Road, and 13 miles to the park entry. Highway 120 travels through the entire park and merges with Tioga Pass Road and far eastern gate at Tuolumne Meadows. Highway 120 ends at the US 395 east junction between Mono Lake and Lee Vining.

Western Entrance – The El Portal Arch Rock entry following State Highway 140 is the most popular entrance entry to the park. It is 75 miles northeast of Merced via State Highway 99 to El Portal and follows the edge of the scenic Merced River seven miles into Yosemite Valley.

Southern Entrance – At the downtown Oakhurst termnius of Highway 49, Highway 41 travels 37 miles east to Wawona Road and the Yosemite Southern Gate and Mariposa Grove of Sequoia Redwoods. At the gate, walk one mile to Mariposa Grove to see the world's oldest living Giant Sequoia, the Grizzly Giant, estimated at 2,900 years old. Wawona Road leds to the Wawona Hotel and restaurant, gas, groceries, Sierra Golf Resort, History Center and central parking.

Eastern Entrance – Limited between December through May for seasonal-only traffic, the Tioga Pass beginning at US 395 reaches the Yosemite Park entry at the Tuolumne Meadows Gate and high-elevation roads ascending to 9,000 feet with many trailheads to mountains, lakes and streams. From there, Yosemite Valley is a several-hour drive via Highway 120.

Yosemite High Sierra Camps & Lodging

Reservations for High Sierra Camps by lottery application are accepted, Oct. 15 to Nov. 30.

<u>White Wolf</u>: 28 cabins and tent cabins   <u>Tuolumne Meadows</u>: 69 tent cabins
<u>High Sierra Camps</u>: 204 beds in 56 tent cabins

Amenities include wood stoves, breakfast, dinners with amenities provided. High Sierra Camps are situated on a loop trail approximately 8 miles apart to 11,516 feet elevation. Guided and independent hikes, saddle and pack trips.

Yosemite Valley
The Ahwahnee: 123 rooms
Yosemite Lodge: 495 rooms and cabins

Wawona
Wawona Hotel: 104 rooms
Housekeeping Camp: 282 units

Yosemite Park Phone Menu	209-372-0200
Camping Reservations	888-530-9796
International Callers	518-885-3639
Wilderness Reservations	209-372-0740
Yosemite Bookstore	209-379-2646
High Sierra Camp Lottery	888-413-8869
Lost and Found	209-379-1002
Medical Clinic	209-372-4637
Room Reservations	559-255-8345
Badger Pass Ski Conditions	209-372-1000
Badger Pass Ski Area	209-372-8430
Saddle and Pack Trip Lottery	209-372-0826
Yosemite Hospitality	209-472-4386
National Park Service	209-372-4726
Cal Trans Highway Info	800-427-7623
Visitor Center, Big Oak Flat	209-379-1899
Visitor Center, Tuolumne Meadows	209-372-0263
Visitor Center, Yosemite Valley	209-372-0299
Visitor Center, Wawona	209-375-9531

A view of Half Dome from Glacier Point reveals the obvious effects of glacial erosion.

Yosemite National Park

Vernal Fall on the Mist Trail is a popular destination for thousands of park visitors.

In March 1851, the Valley of Yo-Semite discovered by the Mariposa Battalion on a pursuit to evict the indigenous mountain tribe, and there to hunt down the lawless Chief Tenaya in a place recognized today as a place of hallowed grounds for peace and preservation. Of the unique forces of nature on display, the ancient scarred granite glaciated faces and polished domes over the Sierra Mountains described by John Muir, radiates from a sun-streaked waterfalls or stream flowing and feeding the Tuolumne and Merced rivers. Traveling to Yosemite National Park offers a range of possibilities.

A national treasure of historical significance within a magnificent 1,200 square miles of parklands, Yosemite covers 747,956 geographic acres of area nearly the size of Rhode Island, with 94.5% of the park's total acreage designated officially as a wilderness preserve. Yosemite Valley's surrounding Giant Sequoia trees, granite domes, mountain vistas, and legendary waterfalls begin with trailheads to hikes into spectacular high country. Yosemite Valley, the most visited section of the park, stretches seven miles by one mile wide. There are 250 miles of roads, 800 miles of hiking trails, around 250 species of birds, 78 species of mammals, and 1,400 species of flowering plants including 37 tree varieties, at elevations averaging 2,000 feet to over 13,000 feet. A center of activity, Yosemite Valley's elegant Ahwahnee Hotel offers fine lodging and dining, as well as a choice for more rustic lodging at Camp Curry inside Yosemite Valley, surrounded by fields of flowers and vibrant waterfalls in view. Within the Valley are suggestions for tours, hiking trails, bicycle rentals, nature walks, a bookstore, winter-to-spring sports, art gallery and native interpretive programs accessible to visitors. Next to the Visitor Center, the Yosemite Museum's Indian Cultural Exhibit, and the Indian Village of the Ahwahnee offer continuous presentations.

Half Dome in Yosemite Valley, during Autumn.

One of the best known locations, the Ahwahnee and Wawona Hotels are each highly-regarded full-service lodging destinations. The rustic setting at Camp Curry lies just below Half Dome and Glacier Point, at the inner Valley's highest edge. Choose from tent camping, standard hotel rooms, and wood cabin accommodations, all by reservations. Although Abraham Lincoln first declared Yosemite and the Mariposa Grove under the public trust of California as parkland, it was considered a part of the national preservation effort from the beginning. Park laws guarding the land against avid 49ers in their search for gold and timber harvesting in the Sierra Nevada lasted through the 1850s. Yosemite was established in 1890 as America's third National Park and supported by the encouragement of John Muir, Robert Underwood Johnson, and pioneer preservationists. A native Yokut Indian term meaning 'the people of Ahwahnee' probably refers to the seeds of the grassy valley they inhabited during ancient times. The Ahwahnee Hotel was completed in 1928 when statistics increased from 60,906 visitors in 1920 to 461,257 in 1929. At first, motor vehicles were allowed to run rampantly throughout the woods and created the main task for the necessary crowd control by Rangers during the nascent years of the National Park Service, established in 1917.

From any section of the Valley floor as a starting point, the convenience of walking, running, biking, and visiting traditional buildings, shops, and museums are surrounded at the edges by trailheads and well-known landmarks such as El Capitan,

Sundown shining on El Cap's granite face.

A 500-foot descent from Highway 120, on the trail to the Tuolumne Grove is a special treat for back-country skiiers.

More than 200 feet tall, the age of the Grizzly Giant Sequoia Tree is estimated to be near 3,000 years old.

Half Dome, Bridalveil Fall, Yosemite Falls, Sentinel Dome, and Glacier Point. Both Vernal Fall and Nevada Fall are accessible inside the Valley from the Mist Trail with scenic landscapes within miles revealing the towering waterfall from the trail. Four-Mile Trail and Panorama Trail begin in Yosemite Valley and lead to hikes and spectacular paths towards Pohono, Glacier, and Inspiration Point.

High above Yosemite Valley, the Tenaya Glacier's imprint with visible striations on the granite-walled canyons open into long views of ultra-smooth polished granite domes and steep monolithic rocks along the horizon. John Muir's findings describe the ecology of glaciers conclusively proving characteristics of Yosemite, and adding contemporaneously knowledge shared by many of the foremost geologists. Glacial evidence throughout the country has been observed in New York's Central Park. Hikes around Tenaya Lake lead towards canyons with visible evidence of glaciation. From the Pohono Trail on the rim above the Valley, Glacier Point Road leads to several alpine meadows of wildflowers near Taft and Inspiration Point, well above the Valley floor. A hike from the rim to the top of Sentinel Dome allows distant views of the Bridal Veil Fall across the Valley Floor. Upper Yosemite Falls and the higher Tuolumne Meadows trails are accessed from Yosemite Valley with permitted high-country hiking for hours in one day or several days at a time at a first come and first served basis, currently by lottery, and two weeks in advance. Unreserved permits are available up to nine days in advance. Visitors to the park setting are guaranteed unforgettable moments viewing natural landscapes and finding scenes of great photography along the memorable trails with panoramic views. Seasonal weather adds ever-changing patterns of storms over raging mountain streams and flooded meadows, and rain and snow dustings appear over the upper Sierra Nevada peaks. A climb up Half Dome is a steady push of eight miles upward one way, with elevations of almost 5,000 feet, and considered a must-do by hikers. At dawn, carrying a well-stocked backpack, water, rain gear, and gloves prepare for the last 900 feet gripping steel cables up a ladder for the most daunting and exhilarating view, always well worth the climb.

During Winter, Yosemite activities include ice skating at Curry Village and snowcat tours, snowshoe walks, ranger-guided tours, downhill, and cross-country skiing at its best. At Yosemite National Park, Badger Pass is the oldest modern ski area out west opened in 1928. Badger Pass

Half Dome from the Pohono Trail, near Glacier Point.

ski area offers downhill skiing, ski rentals, and restaurants. Skiers enjoy groomed cross-country skiing trails serving beginners to intermediate. Also, skiing on more advanced terrain over marked trails is available for outdoor recreation and a lot of fun in the white stuff. Badger Pass Ski Area is right up the trail from the Valley floor. Serious downhill and cross-country skiers have long known Badger Pass as a full-service ski resort that provides a big emphasis on casual family fun. Trying out the first California ski resort steeped firmly in historical tradition is a must. Park Rangers and staff are genuinely friendly and helpful offering great patience. Badger Pass is a down-home California ski lodge for entertaining families and friends since 1935.

Wawona is four miles from the park's Southern Gate, and another mile to walk into the Mariposa Grove of Giant Sequoias. Galen Clark, a one-time miner discovered the Mariposa Grove and resided in a cabin as the official Guardian there, helping to preserve the oldest trees at the park. The Grizzly Giant, the well-known centerpiece of the Mariposa Grove, is considered the oldest Sequoia Redwood estimated around 2,900 years or more. During early park days, the name Big Tree Station gave way to "Wawona", to honor the Nutchu Indian word for Big Tree. The 1876 Wawona Hotel greets guests with 104 guest rooms, 50 private baths, and an elegant dining room for breakfast, lunch, and dinner with its palatial high ceilings, wooden hallways, guest dining room, hotel rooms outfitted with steam heat and natural air-conditioning, today, as in the earliest days, a true Victorian-style getaway with incredible charm. Wawona Hotel in 1875 was originally a stagecoach stop on the way to Yosemite Valley. In March 1882, the Washburn brothers began their management holdings with 160 acres at the Wawona site and later increased in size to 4,000 acres. While living in a cabin at the original homestead of the park, Galen Clark encouraged the Wawona Hotel's owners to begin Wawona Road to furnish a stage line into Yosemite Valley. At the end of the Victorian era, Clarence Washburn sold the family holdings to the National Park Service including the original Washburn Hotel and a group of seven individual buildings, tennis courts, a golf course, riding stables, and history center, as seen today. One building, The Pavilion was a residence of Thomas Hill and noted painter known for depicting portraits of Yosemite landscapes. During the summer, visitors enjoy using the outdoor swimming pool and putter around the peaceful nine-hole golf course. The Washburns began Yosemite Stage and Turnpike Company serving passengers transiting into the Valley center. Visitors were also riding in horse carriages, and the small touring enterprise grew to a size requiring 700 horses.

The Ahwahnee Hotel, Yosemite Valley.

The Great Lounge at the Ahwahnee treats visitors to relaxing accommodations.

Entry to Yosemite Park from the town of Oakhurst via Highway 41 at the park's southernmost extremity has many conveniences and services for travelers. On Highway 41, stopping at an adventure on the Yosemite Sugar Pine Railroad in Fish Camp creates a pleasant and popular railroading trip, with travelers' supplies and lodging nearby. Oakhurst's Gallery Row offers fine art for anyone to enjoy in unique gift shops and quality galleries. Nowhere in Yosemite Valley is there a more spectacular place to enjoy than the elegantly rustic Ahwahnee Hotel, a name the first residents had given Yosemite Valley. Since 1927, its 99 guest rooms have welcomed visitors with first-class luxury accommodations amidst the Valley's world-class natural splendors.

The Wawona Hotel, in Southern Yosemite.

The massive six-story hotel is an architectural treasure designated as a national historic landmark. The Ahwanhee interior has Native American designs characterized by its furnishings beneath high-timbered ceilings. The stained-glass windows, massive fireplaces, and comfortable sofas in the 77-foot-long Ahwahnee Great Lounge provide a place to enjoy cozy evenings. The grand dining room with floor-to-ceiling windows with 34-foot high sugar pine trestles, surrounds guests with views of outdoor walls of jagged granite, and in the Ahwahnee tradition presenting live classical and popular pianists playing most evenings. The world-class cuisine among spectacular views enhancing any breakfast, lunch, or dinner are Yosemite traditions not to be missed. A pleasant bar and a well-stocked gift shop add to the pleasure. The Ansel Adams Gallery in Yosemite Village provides a fascinating two-hour photography stroll across Yosemite Valley. Walk in the footsteps of Ansel Adams and other famous photographers, and discover the best spots for taking breathtaking pictures. Both beginner and advanced photographers appreciate expert guidance.

The nine-hole Sierra golf course runs adjacent to the Wawona Hotel resort grounds.

Southern Gold Country 197

Taft Point provides an inspirational view of the Valley Floor and the Merced River, from the Pohono Trail.

Picture yourself gliding effortlessly on an outdoor skating rink beneath the spectacle of Half Dome and Glacier Point, a must-do for Curry Village visitors of all ages. The rink is open all winter for day and evening sessions, and skate rentals are available. Enjoy skating over ice on a moonlight evening, then warm your feet at the toasty fire pit. Selected tent cabins at Curry Village are available during winter months for a more rustic Yosemite accommodation experience. The Lodge at Yosemite Falls offers theater programs featuring local actors portraying Yosemite legends such as John Muir. Check out the current programs during your visit. At the historical Yosemite Chapel, anytime is the right time to plan a special Yosemite event, such as a wedding, reunion, or anniversary celebration. You can't get more romantic than sharing vows followed by a reception at the Ahwahnee Hotel. Quality catering services and a top-shelf staff at Yosemite are ready to make your plan a reality, whether large or small. For further information about Yosemite online with reservations visit www.yosemitepark.com.

Tuolumne River Grand Canyon and Upper Meadows

From Yosemite, Tuolumne Meadows stands poised directly across Hetch Hetchy Valley. The scenic and spectacular sweeping canyonland along the Tuolumne River runs 15 miles from the Tuolumne Meadows and 20 miles due north along a 5,000-foot descent into a majestic gorge, with the greatest elevation a steep decline two miles west of California Falls. John Muir's description cited, "The cascades of sloping falls of the main river are the crowning glory of the Canyon…miles of the river is one wild, exulting, an onrushing mass of snowy purple bloom, spreading over glacial waves of granite without any definite channel, gliding in magnificent silver plumes, dashing and foaming through huge boulder-dams, leaping high in the air in wheel-like whirls." Tuolumne Meadows is a pure pristine valley beginning from the junction of the Dana and Lyell forks forming the Tuolumne River. It is surrounded by some of the tallest peaks in the Sierra Nevada Mountains and leads to many intriguing trails at the very heart of the range. Muir's term 'Range of Light' applies especially as a poignant description of experiencing

At 9,420 foot elevation, Lembert Dome is a short hike from Tuolumne Meadows.

the trails at Tuolumne Meadows. Conness, Dana, Mammoth, and Lyell peaks stand guard at the northeast of the Sierra Nevada. The Cathedral Range, with unique picturesque peaks, protects the southern boundary. Out of the valley floor of Tuolumne Meadows rises Lembert Dome at the lower end entrance to Tuolumne Grand Canyon with the towering Fairview Dome. John Muir's definition of the native term 'Hetch Hetchy' depicted an edible grass seed once harvested by indigenous Indians of the region. The deep Hetch Hetchy Valley, spelled out 'Hatchatachie', was discovered in 1850 by Joseph Screech while he hunted game there. Muir later explored the valley with Galen Clark in 1875 as fellow guardian conservationists.

The Tioga Road

The 'Great Sierra Wagon Road' was completed in 1883 for $61,000 to become today's Tioga Road. It crosses the summit at an elevation of 9,941 feet, dominated in the Southeast by Mount Dana, rising 13,050 feet. A mile or two north of Tioga Pass, the Old Sheepherder Mine was staked out in 1860 and abandoned in 1874 by William Brusky. Mining was expanded at Old Sheepherder Mine by the Great Sierra Consolidated Mining Company of Sonora after 1878 making their headquarters, and renaming it Tioga Mine.

Large amounts of equipment brought into the area came for a road built at great expense in 1881, and Tioga Road completed in 1883 with nearly $300,000 of expenditures, was abandoned before any ore ever had been milled. The mines closed after 1884 and were donated to the US Department of the Interior in 1915, one of the most scenic in California. Extending through the Yosemite boundaries, east to west, State Highway 120 becomes Tioga Pass Road in Tuolumne Meadows and leads all the way to the western Big Oak Flat Yosemite gate, as the road bisects Yosemite Park the entire width. Although, not designated as a State highway Tioga Road dedicated in 1924, honors Stephen Mather, Director of the National Park Service.

On the Pohono Trail, high above Yosemite Valley.

The Yosemite Pack Train furnishes campsites by lottery and supplies High Camps, via horse trails into the park's highlands.

Hutchings House

The Upper Hotel, a canvas-covered structure stood erected near Sentinel Bridge built by Buck Beardsley and Gustavus Hite and replaced later by J.M. Hutchings after visiting there in 1855, and a John Muir contemporary. Hutchings relocated his family to Yosemite during Spring of 1864 and constructed a twenty by sixty-foot two-story frame structure consisting of two large rooms, with an upstairs and a down. The upstairs room became a women's dormitory and the downstairs housed men and boys. Hutchings used cotton cloth doors with some windows at first and muslin partitions between rooms, eventually replacing them with wooden ones. He added lean-tos and porches and continued renovating the place. Many materials were supplied by the lumber milled from a water-powered sawmill built and run by John Muir in 1868, near the foot of Yosemite Falls. A ditch carried the water from Yosemite Creek running the saw blade, and cutting the boards harvested from several toppled trees throughout the Valley either dead, swept away, or downed during floods and windstorms. A small lawn and scattered shade trees with large boulders, hitching posts, and rails, dominated the scene between 'Hutchings House' and the swift Merced River. Enlarging the place, Mr. Hutchings added a combination kitchen with sitting rooms to the rear. He built a large dirt floor and enclosed a 175-foot tall incense cedar tree applying the name 'Big Tree Room' to this addition. The author, Helen Hunt Jackson, visited the establishment, commenting…"he who would like to open his eyes every morning on the full shining of the great Yosemite Fall; to lie in bed, and from his very pillow watch it sway to right and left under moonlight beams…look down into the amber and green Merced (River) which caresses his very door sill; to listen at all hours to the grand violin-cello tones of the mysterious waters… ask, as we did, in the Cottage for back bedrooms by the River. But, if he is disconcerted by the fact that his bedroom floor is of rough pine boards, and his bedroom walls of thin laths, covered with unbleached cotton; that he has neither chair, nor table, nor pitcher; that his washbowl is a shallow tin pan, and that all the water he wants he must dip in a tin pint from a barrel out in the hall; that his bed is a sack stuffed with ferns, his one window has no curtain and his door no key……let him leave Ah-wah-ne the next day."

Two bucks meet on the Pohono Trail.

TRAILS AND WATERFALLS

In 1865, James McCauley, from Ireland settled at Hite's Cove and mined in the Foothills. Entering into a contractual agreement in 1871 with the Yosemite commissioners, he built a toll trail from the southern end of the Yosemite Valley floor on up to Glacier Point. Another of the most famous trail builders in Yosemite, John Conway, created the rim access. McCauley and Conway accomplished making a new trail in late November 1871, when a heavy snowfall halted work. In the spring continuing into early summer, they finished the Four Mile trail to Union Point. In the 1920s, the Park Service still retains its historic name, although slightly rerouted the trail changing the grade to nearly five miles. An enactment purchasing all trails in Yosemite Valley and the Mariposa Grove in March 1881, made appropriations of $25,000 from the State Treasury and deleted all other toll trails within Yosemite owned by private individuals. In 1882, the State purchased the Four Mile Trail from McCauley for $2,500 and made it toll-free. The old trail begins at the Valley floor and proceeds through five switchbacks at the base of Sentinel Rock, with the present trail up the Talus slope. From there to Union Point, the trail zigzags east and southwest, and is a prime example of demonstrating Conway's engineering capabilities. Union Point, 2,314 feet above the floor of the Valley, allows views of Yosemite Falls, Half Dome, North Dome, El Capitan, Cathedral Rock and Spires while standing there, as well as Big Oak Flat and Wawona roads from in the south.

Scaling vertical granite cliffs are a traditional sport at Yosemite.

YOSEMITE WATERFALLS

BRIDALVEIL FALL	620 FEET (190 M)
CALIFORNIA FALL	20 FEET (37 M) 2: (184 M)
CHILNUALNA FALLS	690 FEET (210 M)
HORSETAIL FALL	2,100 FEET (640 M)
ILLILOUETTE FALL	370 FEET (110 M)
LEHAMITE FALLS	1,180 FEET (360 M)
LECONTE FALLS	229 FEET (70 M)
NEVADA FALL	594 FEET (181 M)
PYWIACK CASCADE	600 FEET (180 M)
QUAKING ASPEN FALLS	25 FEET (7.6 M)
RIBBON FALL	1,612 FEET (491 M)
ROYAL ARCH CASCADE	1,250 FEET (380 M)
SENTINEL FALL	1,920 FEET (590 M)
SILVER STRAND FALLS	574 FEET (175 M)
SNOW CREEK FALLS	2,140 FEET (650 M)
STAIRCASE FALLS	1,020 FEET (310 M)
THREE CHUTE FALLS	80 FEET (24 M)
TUEEULALA FALLS	840 FEET (260 M)
TUOLUMNE FALL	100 FEET (30 M) 2:(179 M)
VERNAL FALL	317 FEET (97 M)
WAPAMA FALLS	1,700 FEET (520 M)
WATERWHEEL FALLS	300 FEET (91 M)
WHITE CASCADE	75 FEET (23 M) 2: (179 M)
WILDCAT FALLS	630 FEET (190 M)
YOSEMITE FALLS	2,425 FEET (739 M)

Yosemite's Bridalveil Fall flows through the seasons, and windy days offer cool refreshing mists spraying the unsuspecting visitors below.

Yosemite Fall and Eagle Peak Trail

John Conway started a Yosemite Falls equestrian toll trail in 1873 and completed it at the foot of Upper Yosemite Fall. By 1877, the trail reached the top of the North rim, and in 1888 at Eagle Peak. The Board of Yosemite Commissioners declared trails and roads in the Valley toll-free except for the Eagle Point Trail whose owner refused eminent domain orders, but Conway, at last was persuaded to sell it in 1885, and paid $1,500.

Ledge Trail

In 1871, James Hutchings guided parties of hikers over hazardous routes climbing vertically 3,200 feet, then blazed a one and one-half mile switchback at the rear of Camp Curry to Glacier Point. Because of hazards connected with the dangers of canyon rock cave-ins, the National Park Service refused to recognize this as an official trail and discontinued its maintenance.

Established in Yosemite Valley in 1899, visitors are served with lodging, food and supplies at Camp Curry and Curry Village.

POHONO TRAIL – RIM TRAIL
The route appeared as the 13-mile Pohono Trail on an 1896 map, originally an Indian path from Yosemite Valley towards the top rim, passes Old Inspiration Point. The Rim Trail, native for 'Pohono' was constructed first during the 1890s, then after 1905 taken over by the US Cavalry. Around 1906, the trail's name changed from Dewey Trail to Pohono and follows the Valley rim, south near Sentinel Dome, and dramatic views of the Valley floor from the 'Fissures' deep rock clefts near Taft Point. The trail continues behind Bridalveil Fall to Dewey, Stanford, and Glacier Points, along the old stage road and ends at Fort Monroe. It joins the earliest trail at the South Fork of the Merced from Wawona Road.

ALDER CREEK TRAIL
One of the oldest trails. 15-miles long and an early main route to Yosemite, Alder Creek Trail leads through Wawona and southern entry near Empire Meadow across the headwaters of Alder Creek along the level trail to Westfall and Peregoy meadows, eventually joining the Pohono Trail. One may turn either left into the Valley to Old Inspiration Point roughly over the route of the original Pohono Trail or turn right toward Glacier Point. Visitors find optimal hiking days during Springtime in May into the Fall Foliage season.

OLMSTED POINT
Tioga Road at Tenaya Lake offers stunning views with moderate hikes from Olmsted Point and access trails with Clouds Rest, Tenaya Canyon, and Half Dome in the horizon. Several trails in this area rank highly with vistas of glaciated granite domes, canyons, and streams spilling into Yosemite Valley.

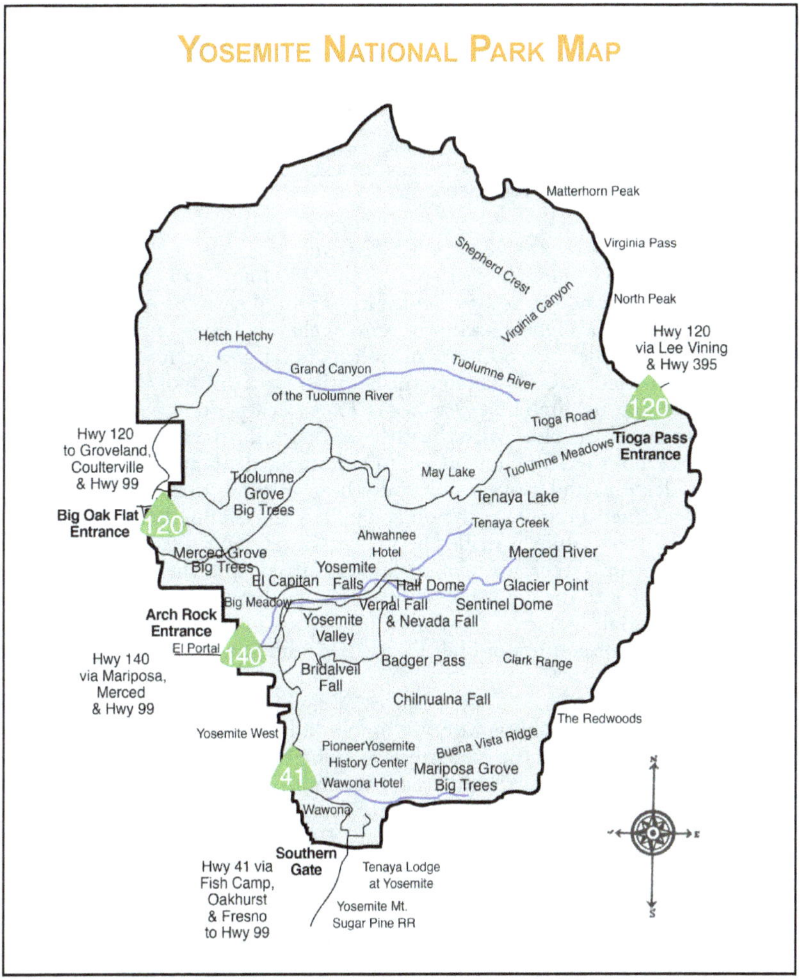

Southern Gold Country

YOSEMITE NATIONAL PARK MAP

- Matterhorn Peak
- Virginia Pass
- North Peak
- Shepherd Crest
- Virginia Canyon
- Hetch Hetchy
- Tuolumne River
- Grand Canyon of the Tuolumne River
- Tioga Road
- Hwy 120 via Lee Vining & Hwy 395
- 120 Tioga Pass Entrance
- Hwy 120 to Groveland, Coulterville & Hwy 99
- Tuolumne Grove Big Trees
- May Lake
- Tuolumne Meadows
- Big Oak Flat Entrance 120
- Tenaya Lake
- Merced Grove Big Trees
- Ahwahnee Hotel
- Tenaya Creek
- Merced River
- El Capitan
- Yosemite Falls
- Half Dome
- Glacier Point
- Big Meadow
- Vernal Fall & Nevada Fall
- Sentinel Dome
- Arch Rock Entrance
- Yosemite Valley
- El Portal 140
- Hwy 140 via Mariposa, Merced & Hwy 99
- Bridalveil Fall
- Badger Pass
- Clark Range
- Chilnualna Fall
- Yosemite West
- The Redwoods
- Pioneer Yosemite History Center
- Buena Vista Ridge
- Mariposa Grove Big Trees
- Wawona Hotel
- 41
- Wawona
- Southern Gate
- Hwy 41 via Fish Camp, Oakhurst & Fresno to Hwy 99
- Tenaya Lodge at Yosemite
- Yosemite Mt. Sugar Pine RR

205

View of Bridalveil Fall centered at the background across from 'The Fissures' on the eastern rim above Yosemite Valley, near Taft Point.

Clouds Rest and Half Dome South Trails

The original trail to Clouds Rest was part of the old Mono Trail of 1882, and by 1912, the commissioners recommended its improvement. The rebuilt spur trail at the base of Half Dome used by several, including James Hutchings, had attempted to scale the 8,892-foot monolith of Half Dome. It seemed impossible until George C. Anderson, the Scottish blacksmith of Yosemite Valley was the first to climb it in October 1875. As a carpenter and former seaman prominently involved with the early trail-building days of Yosemite, Anderson accomplished his climb of Half Dome using drills and a hammer. Driving wooden pins and iron eye bolts into the granite five to six feet apart, he successively fastened a rope to each bolt and pulled himself up, then rested his foot on the last spike while he drilled holes over the next 975 feet to the top of Half Dome. Within a week, six men, including Galen Clark, then age 61, and one woman made it to the top using Anderson's rope. John Muir was the ninth person to climb Half Dome on November 10, 1875. Anderson's plan to build a staircase to reach the summit of Half Dome died with him in 1884.

The cable Anderson fastened to the bolts, enabling Half Dome to be scaled had survived a few years with none other to follow. During the winter of 1883-84, sliding ice ripped the cable from its eyebolts breaking the rope. Several mountaineers duplicated the original climb, replacing the rope in 1895 and again in 1901. Park Supervisor Gabriel Sovulewski recalled Paul Segall replacing the old pegs in 1908. John Muir, in 1910, reacted to the attempt to carry out Anderson's plan to make Half Dome accessible. "For my part, I should prefer leaving it in pure wildness, though after all, no great damage could be done by tramping over it. The surface would be strewn with tin cans and bottles, but the winter gales would blow the rubbish away.... Blue Jays and Clark Crows have trod the Dome for many a day, and so have beetles

A dramatic Winter weather Tunnel View of El Capitan and Half Dome profiles standing across the canyon of Yosemite Valley.

and chipmunks, and Tissiack would hardly be more 'conquered' or spoiled should man be added to her list of visitors. His louder scream and heavier scrambling would not stir a line of her countenance."

THE YOSEMITE CHAPEL

At the edge of a meadow, the Yosemite Valley Chapel built in 1879, is now the oldest original structure remaining in Yosemite Valley. Once standing in the Lower Village in 1901, the Chapel moved to its present location surrounded by spectacular views of granite cliffs, and an impressive view across to Yosemite Falls. The San Francisco designer and architect Charles Geddes created the design as an architectural example of construction in the Sierra Nevada region in the carpenter gothic style found in early mining areas. In 1973, the Chapel entered the prestigious National Register of Historic Places as a nondenominational church open to the public.

Vernal Fall and Mist Trail

The Vernal Fall Trail beginning near Happy Isles in Yosemite Valley follows the south bank of the Merced Canyon near Clark Point to Vernal Fall. When there, one take the Mist Trail to avoids steeper, higher cliffs, on the way to Vernal and Nevada Fall. A fork following the Merced River Trail is a historic trail of 1864. At the top of Vernal Fall, along the south side of the Merced River, an early Indian trail gains access to Little Yosemite Valley. Stephen M. Cunningham made the early trails at the Vernal-Nevada Falls area. Originally from New York State, he was a justice of the peace for Mariposa in 1852 and a business associate of James Savage, the settler of the El Portal trading post. After serving in the Civil War, he returned to Yosemite Valley and Mariposa Grove and became a guide and curio seller. Above

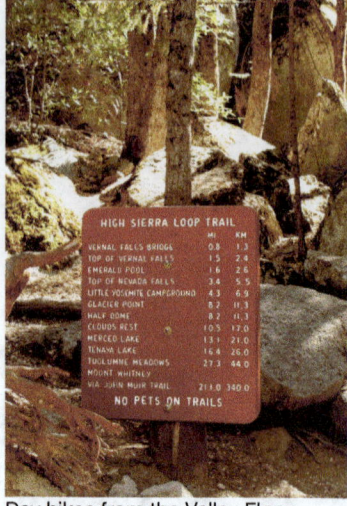

Day hikes from the Valley Floor follow many landmark trails.

the present-day Vernal Fall bridge at the top, The Vernal Fall Trail toll house, although no longer, measured twenty feet long by fourteen feet wide and stood under the edge of an immense overhang of granite called Register Rock, using the overhanging stone back wall as part of the house and making half the roof. That same boulder sheltered a livery stable and other outbuildings.

Snow Trail

In 1870, Albert Snow, the first known trail builder in Yosemite Valley, constructed a horse trail from the Valley floor to Register Rock at the beginning of the Mist Trail over a flat between Vernal and Nevada Falls, where he constructed a hotel. The route of the original trail zigzags to the higher Clark Point turning down to Silver Apron, at a junction just above Register Rock. Then, crossing the bridge near Silver Apron and venturing to the right begins a trail leading directly to the original site of La Casa Nevada. From there to Emerald Pool on part of George Anderson's fabled unfinished trail, from Happy Isles and Curry Village to the top rim.

A stop on a back-country ski trail at the Tuolumne Giant Sequoia Grove, on State Highway 120.

Spring's seasonal runoff at Nevada Fall.

ANDERSON TRAIL

In 1882, George C. Anderson was the first to climb Half Dome in October 1875 and later contracted with the Yosemite commissioners to begin construction on a trail up the north bank of the Merced River, from Happy Isles Bridge to Vernal Fall. Originally planning to build the trail up the north side to the top of the falls in 1885, the commissioners had another connection built from a point on Anderson's trail, uphill to a new bridge below Vernal Fall crossing at the Snow Trail.

PANORAMA TRAIL

In 1871, John Conway laid out a horse trail in the park starting from a point on Snow's hotel site trail to the top of Nevada Fall towards Little Yosemite Valley, along the north side of the Merced River. Washburn and McCready built the original trail from Glacier Point toward Nevada Fall in 1872, following Illilouette Ridge, then dropping to join the Mono Trail at the bridge in Little Yosemite Valley. The 1885 Echo Wall Trail section of the Panorama Trail towards Glacier Point is directly past Nevada Fall. It became the Eleven-Mile or Long Trail. In 1893, the commissioners' report stated rebuilding Panorama Trail with a bridge over Illilouette Creek after long disuse.

A timid Blue Grouse scurries across the forest floor.

Madera County
Historical and Recreational Spots

Oakhurst & State Highway 41
At the junction of State Highways 49 and 41 on day trips from Oakhurst, take a step back to 1870 at a glimpse into the settler lives in California at the Fresno Flats Historical Park. A mining and lumber center serving pioneer 49ers for decades, the town of Oakhurst has today all the needs for recreational hiking and biking with choices of chain markets, vintage, traditional, and modern lodging, remote B&Bs, vacation rentals, and a change of pace in luxury casino lodging. At the termnius in downtown Oakhurst, from Highway 49 at Highway 41 the road takes the trip 37 miles east, and reaches the Yosemite Southern Gate at the Mariposa Grove of Sequoia Redwoods and Wawona Road.

Lewis Creek National Recreational Trail
Lewis Creek National Recreational Trail is a beautiful and peaceful trail following the old route of the historical Madera Sugar Pine lumber flume passing the 80-foot high Corlieu Falls, the smaller Red Rock Falls over and along Lewis Fork Creek. The 3.5-mile trail is located along Highway 41 north of Oakhurst, 5 miles from the South Gate of Yosemite Park.

Fish Camp
The Mammoth Pool Reservoir renowned for fishing off Highway 41 runs along the San Joaquin River. The Kelty Meadow Campground near Fresno Dome has a 1.6-mile hike taking in rewarding views of wildlife and the San Joaquin Valley. Yosemite Mt. Sugar Pine Railroad and Museum is a favorite stopover for an authentic adventure in California on a historic railroad once active during the expansion of logging and mining in the region. Just south of Yosemite National Park, travelers thrill to taking train rides and the sights and sounds of a turn of the century full-sized steam-powered narrow gauge locomotive and railroading experience excursion through the Sierra National Forest using the tracks of old logging trains. The Thornberry Museum, an 1856 homestead cabin, houses artifacts from the pioneer days of the Central Sierra. The train depot is near Yosemite's South Gate off Highway 41 in Fish Camp, 559-683-7273.

Nelder Grove
Nelder Grove, a 1,540-acre stand of Giant Sequoias just outside Yosemite, and The Shadow of the Giants Recreational Trail located within the Nelder Grove of Giant Sequoia. From Highway 41, take the Sky Ranch Road turn and follow the signs about 6 miles to Nelder Grove. Then, take the left fork to the Shadow of the Giants Trail. Willow Creek Trail offers a 2.5-mile hike.

Bass Lake
Nearly 1,200 surface acres or 2.5 sq. mi., Bass Lake was designed in 1901 as a hydro source for a local power company. At a 3,300-foot elevation and 4.5 miles southeast of Yosemite Forks from Highway 41, off Road 222. Pines Resort is a traditional vacation destination at Bass Lake and the adjacent lakeside town, offering restaurant dining, water sports, and vacation rentals. The resort is 14

In a spectacular setting, the Pines at Bass Lake offers vacation rentals providing a full service restaurant, boating slips, and water sports.

miles from the Yosemite southern gate. The water temperature in the lake rises to 80° during warmer months.

WILLOW CREEK TRAIL
Willow Creek Trail offers a 2.5-mile hike first was known to the native American Chukchansi inhabiting the area for thousands of years. Neighboring Crane Valley migrating herons and egrets flock to a tributary of the San Joaquin River at Willow Creek. At Bass Lake, from a moderate to difficult 2.5 miles hike, passes Angel Falls with quiet pools and panoramic views, ending at McLeod Flat Road. Safety measures suggested include being aware of slippery rocks and the dangers of swirling pools. The Trailhead is 2 miles west of the Pines turnoff, along Road 274.

SIERRA NATIONAL FOREST SCENIC BYWAY
A popular 100-mile route for Fall foliage or any time in the year begins along the Sierra Vista Scenic Byway from Highway 41 and gives travelers a closer look at the beauty and spirit of the Sierra National Forest. Follow State Highway 41 and the National Scenic Byway, or 'Hidden Heart of the Sierra', uncovering the rich heritage of the Mono people at the Sierra Mono Indian Museum in North Fork. The Way of The Mono Trail is a half-mile walk into past native history with a study of indigenous natives from the area, the Western Mono Indians. The area has been referred often as being located in the 'Center of California' geographically. The Bass Lake Visitor Center in Bass Lake along Road 222 is the choice of B&Bs, restaurants, and marina docks at the Forks and Pines Resort.

GOLD RUSH HISTORIC PARKS
BODIE STATE HISTORIC PARK
CA-270, BRIDGEPORT, CA 93517

At the 8,379-foot elevation with nearly 200 abandoned buildings, Bodie State Historic Park is among the most significant and authentic 'Second-Era' Gold Rush mining towns in all of California. Today, the park is a well-preserved ghost town 13 miles east of US Highway 395, on State Route 270. Bodie's famed Gold Rush mines between 1876 and 1882 had gained a foreboding reputation of an unabashed paradise and "a sea of sin, lashed by the tempest of lust and passion," in the opinion of Reverend F.M. Warrington. Bodie established the name in 1859 from a partner, E.S. 'Black' Taylor in honor of its founder, William S. Body, who met an early ending there. Ghosts of hardrock mining seemingly hover over the old boomtown in a timeless state that Bill Body, leaving only his name after tragically struck down by a fierce winter snowstorm, still lives on. Explorations yielded $90,000,000 in gold bullion in 1878. Three stages making 18-mile trips daily from Bodie to Bridgeport, and Aurora, Nevada, worked with main economic driver, the Standard Mine and Mill standing today in a state of deterioration along the western Sierra slope, on a bluff overlooking the town. Stages carrying full loads of passengers to towned around to deliver in Sacramento full loads of gold bullion. By 1879, the town counted over 10,000 residents and 2000 buildings. Bodie's devasting fires in 1892, and in 1932 consumed much of the town. The pioneering use of electrical transmission to run the mines was first installed in 1892, and an engineering feat in use well before anyone else. The expansive park is open to the public year-round from 8AM to 7PM, Memorial Day to mid-September, and closes the rest of the year around two hours before sunset at 4PM. 760-616-5040

California State Highway 395
Mono County

Golden Aspen tree foliage intensifies in bright hues along US Highway 395, between Mono Lake and Bodie, a mining Ghost Town.

Mono Lake

US Highway 395, north of San Diego crosses high Sierra mountaintops reaches Carson City in 525 miles. At the Reno Exit, the junction of I-80 leads to Lake Tahoe, and Truckee with all-season Sierra Nevada resorts and several two-lane highways with panoramas and natural landscapes. At Mono Lake, you are surrounded by ancient-looking peaks topped with volcanic craters at the skyline on Highway US 395. The lake's high alkalinity shimmers in an alpine glow at the 6,390-foot elevation in an area of wondrous light and wildlife, and at the center of controversy as a natural source of spring water sent to Los Angeles. The changing ecology of lower lake levels creates an unbalanced effect in the water levels, visually exposing additional natural tufa formations around the lake's rim. These pillar-like abstract forms are produced by calcium carbonate limestone arising underwater when the salty lake water combines calcium-rich deposits in the fresh spring water bubbling up from below. With efforts towards saving its fragility, the Mono Lake Association

Near Tioga Pass and Yosemite, the town of Lee Vining, on US Highway 395 at Mono Lake provides many travel needs for visitors.

at the moment has claimed a victory in the ongoing battle for improvements made by the city of Los Angeles curbing their intake. The effort continues today to protect this precious resource. The primordial water again reflects clear vivid sunsets on the surface where abstract tufa formations are visible on the edges frozen in time. During Springtime, over 300 bird species inhabit the area breeding and nesting, with 85% of the California seagull population migrating to the lake. Lake shrimp and brine flies form a complete food chain, as in the Paiute Indian name for mono, the fly. Mono Lake's two islands, Poaha, the smaller Negit Island, rose to 500 feet above the lake level and were said to have appeared only 300 years ago. The Mono Basin Scenic Area Visitor Center offers elevated outdoor circular views of the area with information kiosks explaining the unique lake's attributes for guests. From US 395, at Lee Vining town center, visit the Mono Lake Committee Headquarters with a fine museum-quality bookstore, local souvenirs, maps for the area, and offers in-depth information. Nearby makes a perfect stopover for a coffee break, or gassing up. Tioga Pass Road, just south, leads to Yosemite Park and the Tuolumne Meadows East Gate.

BODIE GOLD & SILVER MINES

Between Mono Lake and Bridgeport, the once sprawling mining town of Bodie heyday of lucrative mining returns of gold, although, not named 'Bodacious', reflected the town's wild reputation of a mining town tucked away at a frigid 8,379-foot elevation, with a booming in population of around 10,000. By 1879, nearly 2,000 buildings and 65 saloons were in town. However, well before 1940, Bodie was a virtual ghost town abandoned and absent of all life. By 1962, with less than 200 buildings, thousands of artifacts, horse-drawn vehicles, machinery, and domestic accessories, the town remains in hibernation and abandoned in deafening silence. The State of California purchased the land in 1964, and Bodie became a State Historic Park open to the public. The 600 acres in the Bodie Bluffs area east of town added recently to Bodie Gold Rush State Historical Park, and a large National Historic Site and State Historic Landmark, not too easy to reach. A series of twists and bumps leading into the park will jolt almost any vehicle. 760-616-5040

Southern Gold Country

Bright colors reflect at sundown on Mono Lake, in Fall.

GOAT MOUNTAIN LOOKOUT TRAIL
A trail overlooks Bass Lake at the fire lookout 4 miles up a moderate to difficult grade, with great vistas of Sierras and wildlife. There are two trailheads, one at the Forks Campground and the other at the entrance of Spring Cove Campground.

PEELER LAKE
ON THE DIVIDE
Backpacking to Peeler Lake is an 8-mile trip and a rugged 2,500-foot climb. At the top, hikers reach the lake with spillways pouring water down both sides of the Sierra. Its deep clear waters, clumps of mountain hemlock, lodgepole, and whitebark pine set off nearby Crown Point and its campsites. The trailhead lies at the end of a paved 13.5-mile road branching west from US 395 beginning from downtown Bridgeport. For a fee, you can park at the campgrounds at the road's end at Upper Twin Lake. Begin on the trail to Barney Lake and follow signs in the campground.

The Tioga Pass leads to Yosemite National Park's eastern gate, open seasonally.

V. CALIFORNIA GOLD RUSH TO US STATEHOOD
HISTORICAL TIMELINE BETWEEN 1846-1850

Sutter's Fort's 5-acre fortress, as depicted in 1840, was on the Spanish land grant given to John A. Sutter. From Gleason's Pictorial Drawing Room. (Library of Congress)

Spain's conquest of sovereignty over Mexico and Alta California began with their discovery of the New World in 1519. Mexico's war and victory from Spanish dominion in 1821 came with the mission period's decline in California. With American fur traders and tradesmen arriving, the President of Mexico in Mexico City, Gen Mariano Paraedes y Arrillaga, vowed protection of all territories he considered Mexico including Alta California, and the covenant turned to eventual conflicts and skirmishes with the American military, gaining a final victory under the Treaty of Hidalgo signed in 1848.

1846

MAY 13
War begins between the U.S. and Mexico.

JUNE 14
American ranchers ride into Sonoma under the 'Bear Flag Revolt', capturing General Vallejo and declaring independence under the Bear Flag Republic.

JULY 7
Commodore John Sloat lands U.S. Pacific Fleet at Monterey and proclaims California as part of the United States.

OCTOBER
An exceptionally heavy winter traps the immigrant train led by George Donner in the high Sierra.

1847
January 13
Hostilities in California ceased as Captain John Frémont and General Pico sign the Cahuenga Capitulation.

February 10
Frémont is deeded a tract of land near Mariposa, eventually one of the richest locations of the southern mines.

May 16
John Sutter employs James Marshall to choose a site in Coloma on the American River to construct a sawmill.

August 27
Sutter and Marshall sign an agreement to begin construction using Marhsall's know-how.

1848
January 24
California's Gold Discovery was made while James W. Marshall examined the tailrace of the sawmill not yet finished. Marshall notices a glitter in the rocks and suspects he has found gold.

January 28
Meeting back in Sacramento at Sutter's Fort, both Marshall and Sutter are certain about the Gold Discovery.

February 2
The 'Treaty of Guadalupe Hildago' was signed, formally ceding California to the U.S. By mid-February word leaks out about the Gold Discovery.

March 25
The first story of the Gold Discovery printed in a San Francisco newspaper had little attention paid to the report. By late March, John Bidwell visits Coloma and decides to head northwest near Chico. He discovers gold in Butte County.

April 1
Word of the California Gold Discovery reaches the East Coast.

May
800 miners working at Coloma on Mormon Island, Kelseys Diggins, and other areas find rich strikes. Gold claims begin tent camps of Dry Diggins' and North Fork Dry Diggins' with settlements in the Placerville and Auburn areas.

June
The population of Gold Rush prospectors is estimated around 2000-3000.

CALIFORNIA GOLD RUSH AND US STATEHOOD
HISTORICAL TIMELINE BETWEEN 1846-1850

JULY
Nearly 4,000-6,000 miners working in the goldfields hear the gold discovery news had reached worldwide attention.

AUGUST
Rumors reaching the East Coast stir thousands to venture out west. Ships from Hawaii brought prospectors, and word in Northwest Oregon trigger wagon trains south. New mining camps spring up at Jackson, Woods Crossing, Tuttletown, Fiddletown, and Timbuctoo, with Sonorian Camp, the southernmost mining camp settled in 1848.

OCTOBER
Number of miners increased to 83,000 – and, The California Gold Rush begins a dramatic stampede settling the Foothills bringing nearly 300,000 migrants.

1849
In January, the California Gold Rush luring prospectors through San Francisco to the goldfields along Highway 49 covering the north-south route, along the Western Slope of the Sierra Nevada Foothills. A period of discovery begins from "placer" mining sightings, digging out, and panning the gold by hand in the rivers, streams, or exposed cliffs where many undisturbed nuggets had became visible.

GOLD DOUBLE EAGLE OF 1849
James B. Longacre was the designer of the Liberty Head Gold Eagle. The first coin was minted in Philadelphia in 1849 as a golden proof valued at $17 million and stored at the Smithsonian. By 1850, the coins were currency, and the Double Eagle lasted until 1866. During its first years, the coins were struck at the Philadelphia Mint and New Orleans Mint, with San Francisco minting the Longacre Double Eagle by 1855.

1850
Mining transitioned underground into tunnels and mineshafts. The last military governor, Bennett Riley, called a constitutional convention to meet in September 1849 in Colton Hall, at the Alta California capital of Monterey. 48 delegates, mostly pre-1846 American settlers displaced eight native Spanish-speaking Californios. The Convention unanimously outlawed slavery and set up an interim government which operated 10 months before California became ratified for official Statehood by Congress, on September 9, 1850.

VI. Antique Hunting in the Gold Country
Picks N' Pans

The Church Street house kitchen window after the dig.

It's incredible to think lurking beneath one's feet lie uncovered mysteries of the past of the original rough and rugged Gold Rush miners, and pioneer shopkeepers. As California gold-seekers began mining fortunes as an everyday living, the local economy hit paydirt by establishing burgeoning enterprises satisfying the miners' thirst for sodas, beer, whiskey, mineral water, medicinal liniments or medicines. Bottled products were shipped from back East and often packaged in wooden boxes full of colorful hand-blown glass bottles of the day. It's a rare part of American history in shapes, colors, and processes crafting bottles from molten glass blown into molds yielding unlimited forms and translucent colors. Some were odd-looking blob tops, and others used corks or glass stoppers. Soon, smaller factories manufactured up to 1000 bottles daily, and the makers with 4-worker crews rendered bottled products for stocking neighborhood stores and pharmacies with herbal products, condiments, and spirits.

In 2009, an unexpected ring from the old brass doorbell at my Church Street residence and an introduction from a team of curious bottle hunters had mentioned their recent victorious finds right down the block at the Holbrooke Hotel, excavating a giant two-story privy once used by early guests. A pit stop conveniently set up for guests was built in two stories using an elevated walkway connecting the hotel. Once I heard the story, I immediately hoped to find out about the team removing the blacktop from the local hotel parking lot, and made a dig unlike others with over 1000 rare bottles and had left some at the hotel on display. These bottle bounties may had been used once by a US President or famous writer disposing them during their visits to Grass Valley. Laine and John, the bottle hunters were determined in using maps

John and Laine hoist a full bucket of bottles up a vertical hole 15' deep.

from more than 100 years ago made by men hovering above the streets in a hot air balloon and creating survey maps still existing with the plots in Grass Valley, and even my backyard privy! The team's 10-year efforts had achieved local popularity, notoriety, and approval from the surrounding homeowners, as the duo performed what seemed to be a whimsical labor of love to the delight of onlookers unearthing the old town's rare memorabilia from the old red clay.

At my door, Laine explained how he would dig out the top outline and use spring steel six-foot rods to probe into the ground. Soon after, they each agreed once testing it, I had a time capsule buried in the soft embedded material below the Church Street backyard. Quickly, the team launched into a dig at an initial hole width approximately a 5-foot square, to enable one person to dig straight down. The hunt brought buckets of soil out and soon began unearthing a 49er treasure of authentic artifacts of the past! Over the years, Laine, a local building contractor pointed out something most folks overlooked and explained, "it's not only where you dig, but how deep you dig." On this day, the story unfolded into an unexpected prolonged 3-day adventure. It was amazing to know my Church Street residence, after the Civil War was so active upon seeing those paltry discards potentially throw aways by visitors like Mark Twain, Bret Harte, or Herbert Hoover, well beneath where I was standing.

After beginning the initial outline, Laine remarked, "Many recovered bottles are indications of the time they spent

Of the hoard of bottles from the 1800s brought to the light of day were two large Sacramento ale bottles, also medicine, condiment and a rare 2" opium bottle.

underground, as well as teach us how people lived. The bottom layer is probably the 1860s, another layer above from 1870s, and on up to 1890s." Exploring the miniature-sized Church Street backyard was a real surprise because of its limited space. Then, Laine and John discovered a second shaft adjacent to the first, finding the previous owners had expanded digging another hole. Suddenly, our little archeology exercise turned into an unexpected 3-day dig and yielded 200 bottles of many varieties of shapes and sizes. The second hole was just a foot away and revealed a later deeper 1870s–90s shaft descending 15 feet straight down. Once the earthen walls were visible, old original toe-holds used by the laborers became apparent in the red clay sides of the hole with more than 100 years of the earth's stabilization.

An attractive bounty of colored glass was hosed off and cleaned, and the team's ladder lowered for the final dig below the ground level, over four feet further down the length of the 10-foot ladder! With persistent teamwork, they struck bottom and were paid off with an array of bright bottle booty, again visible to rays of brilliant sunlight! The team unearthed bottles from the 1860s through the 1890s, most made back East and some specific ones from California. We brought up two examples of clear 'Loutzenheiser'

glass pharmacy bottles originally used at the old brick building in Grass Valley on Main Street just a few blocks away, and now a town florist shop at its present-day corner location. A brass plaque there describes the 1850s business where it sold pharmaceuticals. Many bottles came with or without embossed art or lettering, when Laine and John explained how "most bottles were hand blown into pre-shaped molds, then impressed by a 'slug plate' that imprinted ornate raised lettering." During the dig, they brought up several tan salt-glazed imported ceramic stoneware mineral water bottles made in 19th-century Bavarian, with some larger wine bottles, deep green champaign splits, and miscellaneous broken shards of glass, as well as condiments, medicine, liquor, and beer bottles. The journey of Grass Valley's

An old 3" tall apothecary bottle.

bottle hunters was indeed satisfied in capturing an elusive Gold Rush bounty in the modern-day world. We even had our hands on a famous 'Pumpkin Seed Bottle', a few Root Beer and Sarsaparilla bottles, a whiskey flask or two, and several herbal remedies making the Gold Country dig a fun-filled thrill by discovering a link to 49er pioneers and once-in-a-lifetime modern day buried treasure!

Guide to Gold Panning

Woods Creek in Jamestown is a delight for young gold miners and older pros.

The Rainbow Connection

The flowing waters from the Sierra Mountains always make great fun for kids, adults, or anyone with the perspicacity to discover something new while wading in the water of the great outdoors through the courtesy of Mother Nature! Gold prospecting is legal on most public lands. It easily can be an absolute investment of time, energy, and persistence, but each attribute assists in finding California gold. First, pondering all the loose nuggets or placer gold already removed over many years. On the other hand, and not surprisingly, some folks still discover large nuggets now and again. Gold in the Mother Lode runs through quartz veins in granite, with phyllite, schist, slate, and greenstone. Then, one may consider recent finds like the 'Butte Nugget' found in 2014 weighed in at 6.07 ounces and was dug out by a gold prospector somewhere in California using a metal detector. The Butte Nugget sold for around $350,000. Another massive mineral rock is the 54 lb. 'The Magalia Nugget' from Butte County dug out with a shovel in 1859. Many eggshell-smooth nuggets remain hidden or submersed while subjected to centuries of the friction from water, leaving a slick golden sheen. Another valuable find cashed in for $10,000,000 from a cache of original gold coinage, discovered serendipitously in a couple's backyard, had been buried in the Sierra Foothills!

The longest single span covered bridge in the country, the Yuba River's Bridgeport Bridge during Gold Rush days charged hog owners paid 5 cents per hog, $6 to cross with an eight horse, mule, or oxen wagon. A one-horse buggy paid $1. Horseback riders paid 50 cents, and people on foot paid 25 cents.

Panning for Gold

Gold flakes and nuggets eroding in the streams are carried off by spring runoff each year. A small effort in understanding how to use a gold pan requires locating first the heavier black sands naturally collecting flakes of gold, as both elements are heavier than any surrounding substances. One gathers 'finds' into a pan using a small gold vial to store the flakes, with smaller shiny pieces conveniently removed using an eyedropper. The bedrock characteristics are worthy of an initial inspection to locate where smoothed granite is a poor place to those where more cracks and crevices help trap gold. Begin in a location suited for the physics of how heavy gold settles into a stream bed or erosion in exposed tree roots, clumps of grass, or mosses often submerged when water is higher, or even on the downstream side of logs stuck or buried in sand and gravel. Look for a bend where the water has washed along a riverbank.

Begin filling a pan with gravel and sand at either an inner or outer bend of the river's elbow along a bank where the stream levels out to slow down on steeper runs. Choose any newly formed gravel bar following a heavy runoff. Rough bedrock with many ridges, crevices, and cracks, especially if they are perpendicular and impede the flow, is the best. Look on the downstream side of large boulders in the stream, gravel bars, or 'glory holes' below areas at the bottom of the stream, scoured down to the bedrock. More potential sites include ridges of cracks where bedrock is at the bottom of rivers and streams and below rapids and waterfalls. Cracks in bedrock above the waterline at the edge of the stream, sand, and gravel on the downstream side of boulders, and just above

Young folks enjoy wading in the storied waters of Jamestown's Woods Creek, a place of good fortune and a great learning experience for most anyone interested in finding gold.

the water level are places. Large nuggets may end up almost anywhere due to turbidity or Spring runoff after years of violent storms.

For finding placers, begin with a full pan, then pour off the muddy water and refill the pan. Begin by removing all rocks and rocking the pan so the water becomes clear and leaves the finer-grained aggregate and sand. Agitate the water and sand mix while spilling the water, washing gold flakes and powder loose from the rest of the mixture. Gold and black sand are heaviest and settle to the bottom of the pan. Again, agitate the pan by reducing the movement and begin to tilt it. The gold and sand settled on the bottom curve and allowed pouring off more gravel and all the water. Continue the process until only black sand with the potential gold is left. Try a magnet to pull away black sand, leaving the gold behind. Gold is soft, whereas gold pyrite, mica, and non-valuable minerals are brittle, break, or crumble. The slight weight difference between gold and black sand makes it so you can pan away the sand until what's left is gold. Beware of 'Fools Gold', or shiny golden pieces of lighter weight mica.

STARTING A MINING CLAIM

What is a miner? A miner is actively and diligently pursuing mining activities, full or part-time, including prospecting, exploration, and development of a valuable mineral on a prospect or mining claim by efficient, reasonable, on-site use of invested time or dollars.

What's a Valid Mining Claim?

Under mining laws, the discovery of a valuable mineral deposit must exist where minerals found within the claim's boundaries are justified with the further expenditure of their labor and means with a reasonable prospect of success in developing a valuable mine. Most certainly, "Buyer Beware" is true when purchasing a mining claim because there is a wide margin of error due to a general misunderstanding of the mining laws, outright schemes, and fraudulent misrepresentation by those who are less than honest. The BLM keeps records of the areas locating mining claims or contact mining organizations such as the Western Mining Council for assistance. Once you have found a claim, record a signed duplicate of the location notice with the County recorder with the claim within 90 days of posting the claim. File a copy of your notice of location with the state office with BLM within 90 days of location. The standard location notice form often is found at a local stationery store. There is no limit to the number of claims an individual can file, and each must have an actual physical discovery of a valuable mineral deposit on each claim. The last step in recording a claim requires filing a copy of the location notice in the recorder's office of the county location of the claim. It must include the claim's date, name, location, state, and whether above or underground. The claimant must file a copy of the official record of the notice of location with BLM within 90 days of location. Proof of labor is necessary by the claimant at the claim, and filed yearly.

Bridgeport in Nevada County

The South Yuba River State Park and the South Fork of the Yuba run for long stretches at a near-level riverbank in Bridgeport, a place for visiting its famous wooden covered bridge for riverfront Spring wildflower walks. Panning is allowed on the South Fork in the State Park, from Edwards to Bridgeport to the boundary of Englebright Lake.

Placer County

There are several select gold panning locations to explore near Auburn and Colfax, including some adventurous backroads.
1/ Take the Weimar Cross Roads exit from I-80, turning east on Canyon Way, and left on Ponderosa to the North Fork in the American River Recreation Area. Ponderosa is unpaved after the first few miles. 2/ At Weimar Cross Roads, turn west, and at the end, make a right on Placer Hills Road, then left on Milk Ranch Road, following to the Placer County Bear River Park area. 3/ From I-80, at the

THE 49ER GOLDEN CHAIN OF MINING TOWNS

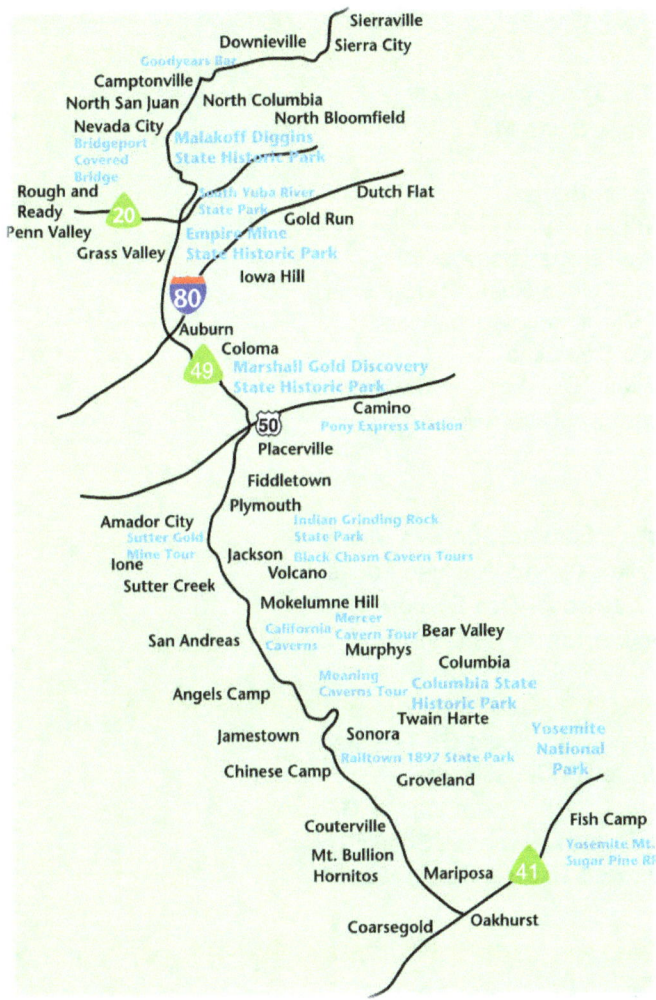

Colfax Exit, turn west, then right on Canyon Way, and left on Iowa Hill Road, proceed to the North Fork part of the American River Recreation Area. 4/ From I-80 at the Colfax Exit, follow the directions to Highway 174 to the Bear River crossing.

WOOD'S CREEK IN TUOLUMNE COUNTY
A lucrative panning area on Highway 49 in Jamestown, Wood's Creek has been the center of attention since the Gold Rush of 1849 and brings school kids, visitors, and prospectors alike to experience the real potential of gold panning. Visit the mining store on Jamestown's main street for directions.

Chapter Index

–14 Tours in the Sierra Nevada Foothills–

California Gold Country Map	... 7
The Golden State Map	... 8
Preface	... 9
Acknowledgments	... 10
Contents	... 12
California State Highway 49	... 19
California Gold Rush State Parks	... 27
Map of California Gold Mines	... 28
The Gold Standard	... 29
1849 Mining Districts of California	... 30
California's Native Americans	... 31

I. Sacramento Gold Country

1. Sutter's Fort to Sutter's Mill	... 37
2. Old Sacramento Walking Tours	... 45
3. Sacramento to Old Folsom	... 61
4. Sacramento to Placerville	... 66

II. Northern Sierra Nevada Foothills

5. Exploring the 'Lake Of The Sky'	... 75
6. Old Auburn Crossroads	... 80
7. Nevada City & Grass Valley Getaway	... 86
8. Yuba Donner National Scenic Byway	... 99
9. Gold Lakes Basin & Sierra Valley	... 116

III. Central Sierra Nevada Foothills

10. Amador Mining & Agriculture	... 133
11. Golden Path Of History	... 151

IV. Southern Sierra Nevada Foothills

12. The Southern Mines	... 167
13. The Yosemite Gateway	... 181
14. Yosemite National Park	... 189

V. CALIFORNIA GOLD RUSH & US STATEHOOD

CALIFORNIA HISTORICAL TIMELINE BETWEEN **1848-1850** ... **216**

VI. PICK AND PANS

GOLD COUNTRY ANTIQUE HUNTING ... **219**
GUIDE TO GOLD PANNING ... **223**

ADDENDUM

CHAPTER INDEX ... **228**
AUTHOR STORYBOARD ... **230**

Autumn foiliage displays above the South Fork of the Yuba River, on Highway 49 at the Independence Trailhead.

AUTHOR STORYBOARD

Within the half-century of living in the Sierra Nevada Foothills and making family excursions over the rigorous curves and steep canyons of California State Highway 49, we encountered the little town of Coloma on the American River and my first impressions of Sutter's Mill and the gold discovery site. Curiosity led to hearing more intriguing stories about the Gold Rush and piqued my interest in documenting those historical places.

On a day hike at Yosemite National Park.

My vision became making personal tours to the original mining towns and discovering the lesser-known places spread out north and south on Highway 49. Closer to home, the very first prospectors traveling by horse and wagon through Marysville using the Henness Pass trail led towards the tent camps of the California and Nevada gold and silver towns in the Sierra. I often followed that same path in making return trips crossing the Yuba River South Fork over the old wooden covered bridge at Bridgeport towards Highway 49, and back to my mountain home on the North San Juan Ridge in Nevada County.

By 1994, I began using my MacSE to established printed guides that addressed Sierra Nevada history, recreation, and events featuring the neighboring mining towns following the Golden Chain. With the advent of digital photography, I created an archive of Sierra Nevada images and made hundreds of meetings at as many places. Regions from the area represent unique getaways, woodland resorts, vintage B&Bs, museums, farm-to-fork restaurants and diversified numbers of recreational businesses within a triangle between Sacramento, Lake Tahoe, and Yosemite connecting more premier travel destinations per square mile probably than almost anywhere. We stand well above the hidden treasures of precious minerals beneath our feet reminding us of the appreciation for our pivotal role in the Golden State's once-in-a-lifetime adventures and discovery along the Western Slope of the Sierra Nevada.

On US Highway 395, the Mono Lake Crater Mountain and extinclt volcanos are visible landmarks on the Sierra Nevada Mountain Range skyline.

The Palm Hotel, at the center of activity near Railtown 1897, and downtown Jamestown on Highway 49.

www.ingramcontent.com/pod-product-compliance
Lightning Source LLC
Chambersburg PA
CBHW052203090526
44583CB00015BA/1254